1983

THE URGE TO LIVE

UNIVERSITY OF NORTH CAROLINA
STUDIES IN THE GERMANIC LANGUAGES
AND LITERATURES

Publication Committee

FREDERIC E. COENEN, EDITOR

WERNER P. FRIEDERICH   GEORGE S. LANE

JOHN G. KUNSTMANN   HERBERT W. REICHERT

30. John Fitzell. THE HERMIT IN GERMAN LITERATURE. (From Lessing to Eichendorff.) 1961. Pp. xiv, 130. Paper $4.50.
31. Heinrich von Kleist. THE BROKEN PITCHER. A Comedy. Translated into English Verse by B. Q. Morgan. 1961. Pp. x, 74. Out of print.
32. Robert W. Linker. MUSIC OF THE MINNESINGERS AND EARLY MEISTERSINGERS. 1962. Pp. xvi, 79. Out of print.
33. Christian Reuter. SCHELMUFFSKY. Translated into English by Wayne Wonderley. 1962. Pp. xiv, 104. Paper $3.50. Cloth $5.00.
34. Werner A. Mueller. THE NIBELUNGENLIED TODAY. 1962. Pp. xi, 99. Out of print.
35. Frank C. Richardson. KLEIST IN FRANCE. 1962. Pp. xii, 211. Paper $5.00.
36. KÖNIG ROTHER. Translated into English Verse by Robert Lichtenstein. With an Introduction. 1962. Pp. xviii, 128. Paper $4.00.
37. John T. Krumpelmann. THE MAIDEN OF ORLEANS. A Romantic Tragedy in Five Acts by Friedrich Schiller. Translated into English in the Verse Forms of the Original German. 2nd Revised Edition. 1962. Pp. xiv, 130. Paper $3.50.
38. Rudolph Hagelstange. BALLAD OF THE BURIED LIFE. Translated into English by Herman Salinger With an Introduction by Charles W. Hoffmann. 1962. Pp. xxii, 106. Paper $3.50.
39. Frederick R. Love. YOUNG NIETZSCHE AND THE WAGNERIAN EXPERIENCE. 1963. Pp. xi, 104. Paper $3.00.
40. William H. McClain. BETWEEN REAL AND IDEAL. The Course of Otto Ludwig's Development as a Narrative Writer. 1963. Pp. x, 109. Paper $3.00.
41. Murray A. and Marian L. Cowie, Editors. THE WORKS OF PETER SCHOTT, 1460-1490. Volume I - Introduction and Text. 1963. Pp. xxxi, 359. Paper $7.50. Cloth $9.00.
42. Herbert W. Reichert and Herman Salinger, Editors. STUDIES IN ARTHUR SCHNITZLER. Centennial commemorative volume. Introduction and Text. 1963. Pp. ix, 117. Out of Print.
43. Clifford A. Bernd. THEODOR STORM'S CRAFT OF FICTION. The Torment of a Narrator. 1963 Pp. xii, 136. Temporarily out of print.
44. J. W. THOMAS. GERMAN VERSE FROM THE 12TH TO THE 20TH CENTURY IN ENGLISH TRANSLATION. 1963. Pp. xiv, 161. Out of print.
45. Phillip H. Rhein. THE URGE TO LIVE. A Comparative Study of Franz Kafka's *Der Prozess* and Albert Canus' *L'Etranger*. 1964. Second printing, 1966. Pp. xii, 124. Cloth $5.00.
46. Edwin H. Zeydel. ECBASIS CUIUSDAM CAPTIVI. ESCAPE OF A CERTAIN CAPTIVE. An Eleventh-Century Latin Beast Epic. Introduction, Text, Translation, Commentary and an Appendix. 1964. Pp. xii, 110. Paper $3.50.
47. E. Allen McCormick. THEODOR STORM'S NOVELLEN. Essays on Literary Technique. 1964. Pp. xii, 183. Paper $4.00.
48. C. N. Stavrou. WHITMAN AND NIETZSCHE. A Comparative Study of their Thought. 1964. Pp. xiv, 233. Paper $5.00. Cloth $6.50.
49. Hermann J. Weigand. THE MAGIC MOUNTAIN. A Study of Thomas Mann's Novel *Der Zauberberg*. 1964. Third printing, 1965. Pp. xii, 184. Cloth $6.00.
50. Randolph J. Klawiter. STEFAN ZWEIG. A BIBLIOGRAPHY. 1965. Pp. xxxviii, 191. Cloth $6.50.
51. John T. Krumpelmann. SOUTHERN SCHOLARS IN GOETHE'S GERMANY. 1965. Pp. xii, 200. Cloth $6.00.
52. Mariana Scott. THE HELIAND. Translated into English from the Old Saxon. 1966. Pp. x, 206. Cloth $6.00.
53. A. E. Zucker. GENERAL DE KALB, LAFAYETTE'S MENTOR. Illustrated. 1966. Pp. x, 253. Cloth $7.00.
54. R. M. Longyear. SCHILLER AND MUSIC. Appr. pp. 200. In press.

For other volumes in this series see page 124.

Foreign Sales through:
Librairie E. Droz
8 Rue Verdaine
Geneva, Switzerland

THE URGE TO LIVE

A Comparative Study of
Franz Kafka's *Der Prozess*
and Albert Camus' *L'Etranger*

by

PHILLIP H. RHEIN

CHAPEL HILL
THE UNIVERSITY OF NORTH CAROLINA PRESS
1964; SECOND PRINTING, 1966

Printed in the United States

NUMBER FORTY-FIVE

UNIVERSITY
OF NORTH CAROLINA
STUDIES IN
THE GERMANIC LANGUAGES
AND LITERATURES

TO RUTH

TABLE OF CONTENTS

IX

PREFACE

There are more than thirty years of an ever-changing century, thousands of years of cultural heritage, and miles of geographical distance separating the lives of Franz Kafka and Albert Camus; yet through art, both of the men explore an experience which gives an exact image of man within the intellectual climate of the twentieth century. They endow their characters with attitudes, feelings, and experiences latent in all men; and they make us, their readers, aware of the anxieties, the isolation, and the anonymity of man in contemporary society. Both artists see man as a stranger bound to an indifferent world: totally responsible for and singly witness to his own existence. As if man were undergoing some amazing trial, Kafka and Camus make the outcome of this trial solely dependent upon the defendant's testimony. From their writings man emerges as an alien in a universe whose illogic and illusions he neither understands nor shares. He is entirely free, solely responsible, wholly guilty, and hopelessly entangled.

CHAPTER I - KAFKA AND CAMUS

The comparison of Kafka's *Der Prozess* with Camus' *L'Etranger* is specifically justified. At precisely the time Camus was reworking his novel, he was keenly interested in Kafka. According to a letter from Camus,[1] he read Kafka's *Der Prozess* in 1938. This is also the year that he reassembled his notes and began to work on the composition of *L'Etranger*.[2] That he was greatly struck by Kafka's work is not only established by his letter, but his impression of Kafka has been given definite form in the essay "L'Espoir et l'absurde dans l'œuvre de Franz Kafka,"[3] as well as in his succinct appraisal of *Der Prozess* in the novel *La Peste*.[4]

For the purpose of this study, Camus' essay on Kafka is undoubtedly the most important single piece of critical writing. This is not to say that the impressive scholarship done on the Kafka problem can be ignored. It is invaluable to any critic who endeavors to substantiate the philosophic and stylistic content of Kafka's writing, and to the comparatist in particular it offers access to the major trends of criticism. In agreement with Wilhelm Emrich,[5] the research done to date can be classified into three main divisions: the theological, the psychoanalytical and the sociological. Any such dogmatic categorizing must of course recognize that there is a great deal of overlapping of positions in these three categories and that in any one critic the major ideas are fused to a degree. What is perhaps more interesting than the grouping of critics within these schools is the fact that any one

1

author's writing can be criticized from so many different points of view. It is at the same time a tribute to and a criticism of Kafka's strength as a creative artist.

The critical writing on Camus is neither as vast nor as diversified as that on Kafka. Since 1942, i.e. the publication of *L'Etranger*, Camus has been regarded by his contemporaries as one of Europe's most significant writers. The 1957 Nobel Prize was an important recognition of the quality of his writing and the climax of his growing international reputation. Although there are critics who take exception to the claim that Camus was Europe's greatest post-World War II novelist, the commentary on Camus' writing reflects general agreement regarding the author's intent. The emphasis placed upon certain facets of the writing varies from the excellent biographical detail of Germaine Brée's book to the stylistic analysis of *L'Etranger* by Jean-Paul Sartre[6]; however, as significant as they may be, the differences of critical opinion center upon the interpretation of specifics rather than upon the central idea of the novels. The critics' opinions vary along with their understanding of Camus' philosophical position.[7]

Although some of these same astute critics have pointed to the derivative Kafkaesque qualities of Camus' writings, no one of them has done an extended comparative treatment of the two authors. The judgments made by such men as Jean-Paul Sartre,[8] Philip Thody,[9] Carl A. Viggiani,[10] and Heinz Politzer[11] are both pointed and

2

interesting; however, a more specific comparison
must be made.

The most obvious point of departure for this
study is Camus' essay on Kafka. In what Camus
refers to as "une interprétation de l'œuvre de
Kafka,"[12] he recognizes the paradoxical and
contradictory nature of Kafka's writing and feels
that the secret of Kafka resides in this fundamental
ambiguity. According to Camus, the perpetual
counter-balancing of the natural with the ordinary,
the individual with the universal, the tragic with
the banal, the absurd with the logical, found
through all of Kafka's work give it its resonance
and its meaning.

The essay, which begins with a characterization
of Kafka's writings as "aventures inquiétantes qui
enlèvent des personnages tremblants et entêtés à
la poursuite de problèmes qu'ils ne formulent
jamais" (p. 174) is divided into three sections.
Within these sections, Camus discusses the specific
use of symbol, absurdity, and hope in Kafka's
works.

Camus finds it extremely difficult to speak of
symbols in writings such as Kafka's, which are
predominantly "natural in quality." The particular quality of naturalness employed by Kafka
is not easily understood. According to Camus,
there are writings in which the events appear
natural to the reader; and less frequently, there are
writings in which the characters find everything
that happens to them to be natural. Through a
singular but evident paradox, the more extra-

3

ordinary the adventures of a character are, the more perceptible the natural qualities of the work will be. "... il est proportionnel à l'écart qu'on peut sentir entre l'étrangeté d'une vie d'homme et la simplicité avec quoi cet homme l'accepte" (pp. 174-175). In order to illustrate his point, Camus discusses Kafka's use of the natural in *Der Prozess* and *Das Schloss*.

He sees *Der Prozess* as a personal expression of Kafka. To a certain degree it is Kafka who speaks and confesses to his reader. The reader is then called upon to project Kafka's spiritual tragedy into a concrete situation. "Et il ne peut le faire qu'au moyen d'un paradoxe perpétuel qui donne aux couleurs le pouvoir d'exprimer le vide et aux gestes quotidiens la force de traduire les ambitions éternelles" (p. 175).

Das Schloss has the same quality of realism. It is above all an individual adventure of a soul in quest of its grace and an adventure of a man who "demande aux objets de ce monde leur royal secret et aux femmes les signes du dieu qui dort en elles" (p. 175). According to Camus, Kafka's secret dwells in this careful balancing of the natural and the extraordinary, the individual and the universal, the tragic and the commonplace, the absurd and the logical. These are the paradoxes which Camus feels must be enumerated and the contradictions which must be underlined in order to understand the absurd work.

Camus develops this idea of ambiguity with a definition of a symbol that is closely related to

4

Baudelaire's definition in "Correspondances." "Un symbole, en effet, suppose deux plans, deux mondes d'idées et de sensations, et un dictionnaire de correspondance entre l'un et l'autre" (p. 176). Camus interprets Kafka's two worlds as the world of the daily life on the one hand and as the world of the supernatural on the other. Just as in life fundamental absurdity and implacable greatness exist simultaneously, the two coincide and play a part in the divorce which separates the soul from the perishable joys of the body. "L'absurde, c'est que ce soit l'âme de ce corps qui le dépasse si démesurément" (p. 177). Since it is only in a game of parallel contrasts that this absurdity can be given form, Kafka expresses tragedy through the commonplace and the absurd through logic.

Camus compares this technique to that employed by the Greek dramatists. By the playwright's announcement of the character's destiny in advance, the entire effort of the drama is to show the logical system which, from deduction to deduction, brings about the hero's misfortune. To announce this judgment is not horrible because it is unreasonable; however, if the necessity of this action is demonstrated in the framework of everyday life, then the horror becomes overbearing. "Dans cette révolte qui secoue l'homme et lui fait dire: 'Cela n'est pas possible', il y a déjà la certitude désespérée que 'cela' se peut" (p. 177).

To Camus, all of Kafka's writings are in this style. Although *Das Schloss* is essentially the struggle of a soul in quest of its grace, the details of

5

daily life are what appear to be emphasized. In *Der Prozess*, the hero could have been named Schmidt or Franz Kafka. He is named Joseph K. He is not Kafka and yet he is Kafka. He is universal. Yet, he is the entity K.

Camus recognizes that Kafka's heroes know in advance that they will gain nothing from their quests and that they allow themselves the torturing luxury of pursuing their goal until death. He believes that the effect of absurdity is clearly bound up with this excess of logic. To him, *Der Prozess* is totally successful as an absurd work in principle. "La chair triomphe. Rien n'y manque, ni la révolte inexprimée (mais c'est elle qui écrit), ni le désespoir lucide et muet (mais c'est lui qui crée), ni cette étonnante liberté d'allure que les personnages du roman respirent jusqu'à la mort finale" (p. 179).

The first division of Camus' criticism is concluded with the above argument. The second section endeavors to prove the thesis that in this universe without progress, Kafka introduces hope in a singular way. In Camus' opinion *Der Prozess* and *Das Schloss* complete one another: "L'insensible progression qu'on peut déceler de l'un à l'autre figure une conquête démesurée dans l'ordre de l'évasion" (p. 180). *Der Prozess* raises a problem which *Das Schloss* solves to a certain degree. *Der Prozess* diagnoses; *Das Schloss* proposes a treatment. Although the remedy proposed does not cure, it aids in the acceptance of the disease. As with Kierkegaard, it makes the disease cherished.

6

This subtle remedy which causes us to love that which crushes us and brings hope into a world without issue is the secret of the existential revolution.

Turning to an analysis of *Das Schloss*, Camus affirms that each chapter is not only a failure but also a rebirth. K. is determined to be accepted by the castle in spite of constant defeat. In his insane hope for acceptance, he abandons morality, logic, and truth. After failing to attain adoption alone, he expends all his effort to merit this grace by becoming a citizen of the village, but again he fails. In his last desperate attempt to gain entry into the castle, he turns to the Barnabas family. According to Camus, the road which K. chooses from Frieda to the Barnabas sisters leads from confiding love to the deification of the absurd. "L'ultime tentative de l'arpenteur, c'est de retrouver Dieu à travers ce qui le nie, de le reconnaître, non selon nos catégories de bonté et de beauté, mais derrière les visages vides et hideux de son indifférence, de son injustice et de sa haine" (p. 183).

In the third and final section of his essay, Camus explains the meaning of hope as it is applicable to *Der Prozess* and *Das Schloss*.

The word hope as applied to Kafka is not ridiculous, for the more tragic the condition reported by Kafka becomes, the more rigid and superrational the hope must be. The more absurd *Der Prozess* is, the more the leap of *Das Schloss* appears moving and illegitimate. This is the pure paradoxical thought of the existentialists as expressed by Kierkegaard: "On doit frapper à mort l'espérance terrestre, c'est alors seulement qu'on se sauve par l'espérance véritable" (p. 184). Applying this statement to Kafka, Camus says that it was necessary for Kafka to have written *Der Prozess* in order to undertake *Das Schloss.*

Most critics have defined Kafka's works as a cry of desperation. This definition, according to Camus, demands revision. There is optimistic hope as expressed by Henri Bordeaux, and there is despair as expressed by Malraux. Neither consists of the same hope nor of the same despair. Only the absurd may lead to the infidelity which Camus seeks to avoid. "L'œuvre qui n'était qu'une répétition sans portée d'une condition stérile, une exaltation clairvoyante du périssable devient ici un berceau d'illusions. Elle explique, elle donne une forme à l'espoir. Le créateur ne peut plus s'en séparer. Elle n'est pas le jeu tragique qu'elle devait être. Elle donne un sens à la vie de l'auteur" (p. 185).

According to Camus, it is strange that the works of kindred inspiration like those of Kafka, Kierkegaard, and Shestov, which have turned completely toward the Absurd and its consequences, terminate with an immense cry of hope. They embrace the God who devours them, and it is through their consequent humility that hope introduces itself. The absurdity of existence assures them of the reality of the supernatural. If the path of this life ends with God, there is, then, a way out. "Kafka

8

refuse à son dieu la grandeur morale, l'évidence, la bonté, la cohérence, mais c'est pour mieux se jeter dans ses bras" (p. 186). Once Kafka resigns himself to the absurdity of the world, we know from this moment that it is no longer the true doctrine of Absurdity to which he adheres. Within the limits of man's condition, no greater hope exists than that which permits him to escape the absurdity of human life and throw himself into the arms of God.

Camus concludes that Kafka's writings are probably not absurd, for in a truly absurd work "... l'ultime message réside dans une lucidité stérile et conquérante et une négation obstinée de toute consolation surnaturelle." (p. 188). According to Camus, Kafka's work is religious in inspiration, and because of this fact, the work is universal. Camus knows and admires this inspiration, but he himself does not seek the universal but the truth. "... je ne cherche pas ce qui est universel, mais ce qui est vrai. Les deux peuvent ne pas coïncider" (p. 187).

Camus' essay is offered as one of several possible interpretations of Kafka's writing. In a concluding note, he states that: "Ce qui est proposé ci-dessus, c'est évidemment une interprétation de l'œuvre de Kafka. Mais il est juste d'ajouter que rien n'empêche de la considérer, en dehors de toute interprétation, sous l'angle purement esthétique" (p. 189). It is interesting that in this study Camus emphasizes Kafka's ability to transport his reader to the confines of human thought; that, giving the word its full meaning, it can be said that everything in Kafka's work is essential; and that, in any case, the writings propose the problem of the absurd in its entirety. These ideas are the expression of Camus' thoughts concerning an author whom he was reading and analyzing at the time he was reworking his original draft of *L'Etranger*. It is certainly more than coincidence that these same ideas are essential to an understanding of that novel.

As in most critical comparisons such as this, much will remain unsaid; however, the points of similarity in these two major twentieth-century writings suffice to justify that degree of limitation. As is clear from any brief survey of his writings, in no other work does Camus approach so closely the confines of a Kafkaesque universe as he does in *L'Etranger*. On many points the basic premise of his total production contrasts sharply with Kafka's artistic outlook. This distinction becomes clear if one imagines Kafka and Camus standing before a curved shop window while admiring a magnificent collection of art objects. Each of them is lost in his own thoughts and oblivious to the bustling of the intersection where the shop is located. At one moment, jolted out of their reveries by a sudden noise, they both lift their eyes and see the grotesquely distorted mass of men and machines as they are reflected in the curved glass. Momentarily, these objects appear to be monstrous phantoms closing in on the two men. Both pause, stare, shudder. Kafka quickly lowers his glance. Camus turns and steps into the street.

10

„Ach", sagte die Maus, „die Welt wird enger mit jedem Tag. Zuerst war sie so breit, dass ich Angst hatte, ich lief weiter und war glücklich, dass ich endlich rechts und links in der Ferne Mauern sah, aber diese langen Mauern eilen so schnell aufeinander zu, dass ich schon im letzten Zimmer bin, und dort im Winkel steht die Falle, in die ich laufe." – „Du musst nur die Laufrichtung ändern", sagte die Katze und frass sie.[13]

Comprendre le monde pour un homme, c'est le réduire à l'humain, le marquer de son sceau.[14]

Der Prozess and *L'Etranger* are unusual works which at first puzzle the reader. Kafka and Camus present a sequence of events that are unmistakable, concretely realized, and plausible; however, at the moment the reader is called upon to fit these events into a logical pattern, he is forced to readjust his position or to regard the novels as absurd. Neither Kafka nor Camus disputes the man of facts; rather by a displacement of time-space relationships, they upset the conception of the world held by the man of facts. Both authors understand that the fictive world must somehow be made real, and that to be made real, it must be depicted with great particularity of detail; but this precision of method is applied to worlds of their own creation. It is only at the point where the reader realizes that he must readjust his position that he is aware that the works are not intended as representations of everyday life but as symbols of man's condition.

Although the action of the novels is primarily symbolic in meaning, these works are objectively presented in every respect. The events, the characters are given. Never are they interpreted. At every moment the reader feels that he is somewhat removed from his everyday world of facts, but at no moment is he able to state definitively that at exactly this point, in exactly this way, the author has rejected realism. Never – even in the most bizarre moments – is a totally unreal interpretation the only possible one. Everything can be logically described, even though it cannot

12

always be known. What has happened here is that although realism is upended, it is never discarded. Kafka and Camus parade the conglomeration of everyday living before the reader. He gets an appearance of work-a-day living: there are men and women leading diverse, insignificant lives in cities that are real in every respect. But on close examination the men and women are types. There is the curious party of three that is on watch during K.'s first moments of trial, and there is the strange little automaton in *L'Etranger* who appears one day at Céleste's and again at the trial. There are the conventionally inexplicable acts of a man being arrested for no obvious guilt and a man being executed for not having wept at his mother's funeral. There are these characters and events, but in the presentation of neither does either Kafka or Camus ever offer an explanation.

Before the reader is entangled in his interpretation of the symbolic meaning of the novels, he is aware of a fictive world that although unlike his own world has many things in common with it. There is realism of detail within a framework of symbolism, and the reader is immediately keenly aware of these details. It is in the artistic presentation of these details, in the use of literary devices to create atmosphere and give meaning to the action of *Der Prozess* and *L'Etranger* that one of the major similarities between Kafka and Camus is discernible. In the significance of time to the protagonists, in the portrayal of characters, in the creation of settings, in the emphasis upon sense impressions, and in the use of counterpoint and irony there are many similarities in the writing of Kafka and Camus.

In both *Der Prozess* and *L'Etranger* the main theme is one of life and death. The novels close with the death of the protagonists and are primarily concerned with the meaning of life which may be ascertained from these deaths. One of the most significant devices employed by the authors to convey their particular meaning is the use of time in relationship to the development of the heroes' thoughts. The opening sentence of *Der Prozess* reads, "Jemand musste Josef K. verleumdet haben, denn ohne dass er etwas Böses getan hätte, wurde er eines Morgens verhaftet" (p. 9). Camus employs a similar technique in *L'Etranger*: "Aujourd'hui, maman est morte. Ou peut-être hier, je ne sais pas."[1] These openings are first an effective employment of the classical doctrine of *in medias res*, which, as a technique, immediately captures the reader's attention. More significant, however, is that the reader is instantly made aware of the importance of time. It is true that the definity of the definite time concepts "Morgen" and "aujourd'hui" is consciously weakened – almost completely lost – by the modifying adjective and phrase: "eines"; "ou peut-être hier"; yet from the beginning a feeling of timelessness within time is conveyed to the reader. And this feeling of timelessness is important, for to Kafka and Camus the themes of their novels are not confined to one particular moment in the history of man.

14

With the one exception of the ninth chapter of *Der Prozess*, "Im Dom," the opening paragraph of every chapter of the novel has some reference to time, such as "am nächsten Sonntag" or "während der nächsten Woche" or "an einem Winter-vormittag." And each event within the chapters takes place at a specified time of day: "Als er um halb zehn Uhr abends vor dem Hause ... ankam" (p. 28); "Etwa bis elf Uhr lag er ruhig" (p. 34); "Allerdings lief er jetzt, um nur möglichst um neun Uhr einzutreffen" (p. 47).

The significance of time is also implicit throughout the first part of *L'Etranger*. Here, too – with the one exception of chapter five – the opening paragraph of each chapter has some reference to time: "c'est aujourd'hui samedi" or "J'ai bien travaillé toute la semaine" or "Le dimanche." And each event within the chapters takes place at a specified time of day: "J'ai pris l'autobus à deux heures" (p. 10); "J'ai dormi jusqu'à dix heures" (p. 34); "A cinq heures" (p. 37); "Je suis sorti un peu tard à midi et demi" (p. 41)[2].

Within this carefully planned framework of time, in which the events of each novel take exactly one year, time suddenly stops and realism is suspended. Time is a necessary and convenient framework that finally disappears, and the reader is placed face to face with a world that has nothing in common with his own. In the chapter "Im Dom," other than for the omission within the first paragraph, the events are narrated with the usual specific time references: "als K. schon um sieben Uhr ins Büro kam" (p. 239); "etwa um zehn Uhr" (p. 242); "Gerade um halb sieben Uhr" (p. 243); "gerade bei seinem Eintritt hatte es zehn geschlagen" (p. 244); and so forth. In fact, time references are so numerous that at the moment time stops, its shriek is almost as loud as the angry cry from the pulpit. Almost every paragraph before the priest delivers his sermon has at least one reference to time: "Jede Stunde"; "die Bürozeit"; "zweitagige Geschäftreise"; "am nächsten Tag"; "für einen Tag"; "Stürmischer Morgen"; "um sieben Uhr"; "die halbe Nacht"; "endlich sah der Italiener auf die Uhr"; "wenig Zeit"; "in zwei Stunden." At exactly eleven o'clock the priest mounts the pulpit to begin his sermon, and a few moments later "das war schon tiefe Nacht" (p. 254). Logically, the black night may be explained by the particular storm that is referred to throughout the chapter; however, from this moment to the end of the chapter there is no mention of time. Time has stopped. Joseph K. is guilty. Time is dead.

As in the cathedral episode of *Der Prozess*, in Part II of *L'Etranger* there is almost a total absence of the mention of specific time. References to specific time are replaced by references to day and night, sky and stars. Meursault never thinks of days as such: "Les mots hier ou demain étaient les seuls qui gardaient un sens pour moi" (p. 115). He refers to the hour of the sunset as "L'heure sans nom" (p. 115), and during the first trying months in prison, his remembrance of the women he had

16

loved – no matter how unsettling – "tuait le temps" (p. 111). One page later he repeats the phrase: "Toute la question, encore une fois, était de tuer le temps." And again on the following page: "Il me restait alors six heures à tuer." As Carl A. Viggiani points out,[3] the whole concept and meaning of time are being killed in and by the hero's experience. After the third restatement of the theme, it appears again:

> J'avais bien lu qu'on finissait par perdre la notion du temps en prison. Mais cela n'avait pas beaucoup de sens pour moi. Je n'avais pas compris à quel point les jours pouvaient être à la fois longs et courts ... tellement distendus qu'ils finissaient par déborder les uns sur les autres... Pour moi, c'était sans cesse le même jour qui déferlait dans ma cellule (pp. 114-115).

After two days of the trial, time has stopped. Meursault is guilty. Time is dead.

In the initial stages of the novels, each of the protagonists' sensations corresponds to one particular moment in time. To K. and Meursault there is no past or future but only a succession of presents. As their characters develop from the particular to the general to the universal, the references to specific time disappear. They are as if momentarily removed from the changeless rhythm of time, and it is in these moments when time is suspended that K. and Meursault begin to evolve

17

from purely sentient consciences to men who see beyond their own ego to their relationships with other men. That time is an integral part of the novels in stucture and theme is obvious.

If one turns from the study of time to the characters' functioning within this time pattern, the most outstanding similarities are found to exist between the central figures of the novels. There is an amazing similarity between Joseph K. and Meursault. There can be no doubt that these faceless office workers represent man in the present age: his fervent desire that the world should be explicable in human terms and his painful awareness that it is not so. They are faceless, for they are intended to represent every man, not one man. On close inspection neither possesses the character of a person of any genuine individuality. Their faces are borrowed faces which they have acquired hurrying through life. Any impression the reader has of them derives from their impact upon other characters within the novels and not from any physical description of them. Through constant movement, they remain anonymous in one respect; yet paradoxically they gain in this anonymity – through the reader's stimulated imagination – an identity with all men.

Joseph K. is thirty and a bachelor, independent and egocentric. His life is beautifully and rightfully coordinated into the bourgeois way-of-life. He dutifully pursues his profession as a bank clerk and daily follows the same monotonous routine. He works in his office until nine in the evening, takes

18

a short walk, drinks beer with his friends until eleven, goes home to his boarding house. He has no obligations other than to himself. His father is dead; his mother is ill and away. What family he does have is of no consequence to him; according to the fragmentary chapter "Fahrt zur Mutter," K. has not seen his mother for three years, and the chapter "Der Onkel" clearly illustrates his indifference to family ties. The only exceptions to his routine are the occasional invitations from the bank manager for a drive or a dinner at his villa and his visit once a week to Elsa – a girl who was on duty all night till early morning as a waitress in a cabaret and during the day received her visitors in bed. Even this love is conducted in a functional, unbinding way. It places no burden on his freedom or his afternoon-off.

In no aspect of his life does K. have any idea of the entanglements that generally surround human existence. Up to the moment of his trial, he is totally unaware of the nullity of an existence of this sort. After the time of arrest until his death, although he is incapable of revolt, there is a gradual development toward an awareness.

Meursault, the main figure of *L'Etranger*, is completely indifferent to everything except physical sensations. He is thirty and a bachelor. He dutifully pursues his profession as a clerk, but he is more interested in the pleasant dryness of a towel in the washroom at midday and its clamminess at night than he is in a possible promotion to Paris. He lives in a succession of presents in which all

19

pleasures are sensual experiences. Smoking, eating, swimming, fornication are all equal acts. Even the death of his mother has no immediate effect upon him. He has no obligations other than to himself. His family is dead and he is alone in a rooming house. He is detached from any of the entanglements that generally surround human existence and he remains so detached until the moment he resigns himself to the benign indifference of the universe.

Both of these fictive creations are beyond good and evil – not because they want to be there, but because they are not capable of recognizing the distinction between good and evil. What remains for them is the fear of having missed the real purpose of life, of having become guilty of leading a misconducted life which can only be atoned for by its own destruction. The development of K.'s and Meursault's initial unawareness of this guilt to alarming awareness is subtly manipulated by Kafka and Camus.

For a time following their arrest K. and Meursault attempt to fit everything that happens to them into the logical framework formed by their own previous experiences. They view their cases with detachment and keep as much as possible beyond immediate contact with them. They allow them to intervene whenever it suits them but are also able to withdraw from them at will. At first it is difficult for either to think of his position as being altered in any way. In speaking of his arrest to Frau Grubach, K. says that he considers the

20

whole acusation of guilt "... nicht einmal für etwas Gelehrtes, sondern überhaupt für nichts" (p. 30). Meursault's position is similar to K.'s, for at the conclusion of his interview with the examining magistrate, a week after his arrest, he remarks on leaving that "... j'allais même lui tendre la main, mais je me suis souvenu à temps que j'avais tué un homme" (p. 92). It is only after a considerable lapse of time that the consciousness of the charges against them gains importance and reality for them. Everyday life gradually appears more and more as an empty course, endured only through habit. The arrest, which had once been easy to dismiss for K., now becomes his sole mental occupation. He is caught in a series of obstructions – seemingly spread into infinity – that involves the cultivation of court officials, an advocate, and a painter. Meursault, too, at first thinking in terms of everyday living, after a period during which he adjusts himself to existing conditions, succumbs to his trial and is able to think of little other than the dawn and his appeal. Both men are caught. At the end of their lives they are finally detached from the vain seeking of the world, and through the experience of approaching death are delivered to their unfilled urge to significance. In the final moments of life they no longer see themselves in the inexhaustible march of time but in the importance of the present moment. It is at this point that the awareness of the changes – brought about within them by the trial – is apparent to them, and it is at this moment that the reader comes to full realization of the symbolic significance of the titles *Der Prozess* and *L'Etranger*. As K. hopes that the shame of his death will outlive him, Meursault longs for cries of execration as he is led to the guillotine. Both have thoughts of beginning again. The reader is forced to. The struggle depicted here is real; the meaning of this struggle is symbolic.

The physical similarities in the development of K. and Meursault are further highlighted by the narrative devices employed by Kafka and Camus. It is necessary that these devices be specified before the minor figures of the novels are compared. Kafka and Camus both employ a classic style that is characterized by extreme objectivity in narration into which the narrator's sentiments are never allowed. In *Der Prozess* the narrator tells the reader what is happening; yet all interpretation is omitted and strictly limited to what is happening in K.'s mind. Everything is seen from K.'s point of view and nothing is related that is not experienced by him. In *L'Etranger* all events are narrated by Meursault. These narrative devices permit both authors to deal with the essence of character and meaning. By restricting the interpretation of all events to the main characters, Kafka and Camus are freed from any deadening photographic quality of realism and are able to concentrate upon the subjective individuality of Joseph K. and Meursault. The characters feel and know and act, and as readers we are permitted to see how they feel and know and act; but our sight is limited by an extremely narrow point of view. K.

22

and Meursault "interpret" the outside occurrences, and their interpretation changes in the course of the works. Above this, however, is the much more subtle "interpretation" of the authors which includes both characters and events. The authors know what the characters, at best, gradually understand. The interpretation of the authors is subtly inherent in the interpretations of the characters. In *Der Prozess* and in *L'Etranger* an unexpected and curious accident suddenly awakens the protagonists to conscience, and another life and another destiny are determined for them by this accident. They perceive that this extraordinary event will no longer permit them to close an eye until they yield to the sleep of death. And as readers we witness the awakening to this new existence through the eyes of the victim. What alterations occur in the characters – however slight they may be – within the framework of the novel are significantly magnified when projected out of the subjective individuality of the protagonists into the objective observance of the reader. Consequently, any development in the individual may take on new significance to the reader while remaining wholly insignificant to K. or Meursault.

The similarity of the narrative devices used by Kafka and Camus in part explains the amazing similarity between the artistic portrayal of the minor characters of these books. Like the curious party of three that watches K. during the first moments of his arrest and the strange little automaton in *L'Etranger*, most of the minor characters are not fully developed.[4] Only certain features are emphasized; however this bold delineation invites our imagination; and soon, as a result of seeing the characters in action, we no longer think of them as mere outlines but are able to perceive a composite whole – a picture of man stripped of his lush, sensual qualities. The seduction of physical beauty is removed, and we are struck by the powerful workings of the inner being of one particular individual at one specific moment in his life. What has gone before this moment or what comes afterward is of no importance. The reader, as are K. and Meursault, is permitted to grasp fleetingly only certain features of a character, and from these few characteristics he must form his opinion. Leni of *Der Prozess* is portrayed in the following way:

Im Guckfenster der Tür erschienen zwei grosse, schwarze Augen ... (p. 121).

Wieder erschienen die Augen, man konnte sie jetzt fast für traurig halten ... (p. 121).

... ein junges Mädchen – K. erkannte die dunklen, ein wenig hervorgewältzten Augen wieder – stand in langer, weisser Schürze im Vorzimmer und hielt eine Kerze in der Hand (p. 122).

... es hatte ein puppenförmig gerundetes Gesicht, nicht nur die bleichen Wangen und das

24

Kinn verliefen rund, auch die Schläfen und die
Stirnränder (p. 122).

... eine kleine Hand ... viel kleiner als K.s
Hand ... (p. 130).

... er ... sah auf ihr reiches, dunkles, fest ge-
drehtes Haar hinab (p. 132).

Sie spannte den Mittel- und Ringfinger ihrer
rechten Hand auseinander, zwischen denen das
Verbindungshäutchen fast bis zum obersten
Gelenk der kurzen Finger reichte (p. 134).

...ging ein bitterer, aufreizender Geruch wie von
Pfeffer von ihr aus ... (p. 135).

Kafka nowhere gives a detailed description of Leni.
The description we have is scattered over several
pages. The reader has a verbal picture of a personality enclosed in a non-described female body
with dark expressive eyes, a doll-like rounded face,
small hands, dark, firmly knotted hair, and a right
hand with a connecting web of skin between the
middle and ring fingers. The details are sharp and
architectural but in no way complete.

In *L'Etranger* Camus describes Raymond Sintès
in much the same way:

Il s'appelle Raymond Sintès. Il est assez petit,
avec de larges épaules et un nez de boxeur. Il est
toujours habillé très correctement (p. 44).

25

Il avait un pantalon bleu et une chemise blanche
à manches courtes. Mais il avait mis un canotier,
ce qui a fait rire Marie, et ses avant-bras étaient
très blancs sous les poils noirs (p. 72).

A short, thick-set man with a nose like a boxer's
and rather hairy forearms: physically this is all
that the reader knows about the man whose actions
are directly responsible for Meursault's trial and
eventual execution.

In spite of the slightness of these verbal sketches
by Kafka and Camus, the reader is never allowed
to feel that he is dealing with unreal people. One
obvious means employed to avoid unreality is the
handling of all the characters in constant
movement. We see them as K. or Meursault sees
them. One particular physical attribute strikes
them at one particular moment: one woman
laughs happily, another is plump and cheerful,
still another presses her open palms on her hips. At
the particular moment to the particular observer
this one aspect is the aspect which overpowers all
others. As a stylistic device these faceless characters serve a double purpose: the protagonists are
placed in flat relief and their egocentricity is
heightened by their inability to see beyond the
obvious.

In keeping with the selection of primary facets
of character and of action, the intensity of the
novels is highlighted by the intensity of the scenes
in which the action takes place. These are novels
that physically as well as mentally confine their

26

protagonists. In *Der Prozess* the sun never shines. K. is ever-surrounded by dull, heavy air that is hardly breathable. During the few moments that he is outside and free from immediate involvement in his trial, rain or snow falls in foggy dimness. At every decisive moment K.'s perception is physically limited. The sultry heat of the court, of the advocate's home, of the artist's apartment stifles him. He is never able to perceive clearly the impact of any event because of the exhausting pressure placed upon him to fight first his physical environment. During his visit to the court, low ceilings where people are only able to stand in a bent position with their heads and backs knocking against the ceiling keep him from making any sensible observation of the court. During his visit to the court offices, K. feels the air too thick for him and stands crushed against the table, feeling as if seasick. During his interview with the advocate, it is too dark for K. to see anything clearly. And again the sultry heat when he visits the artist Titorelli; and again the gloomy darkness in the cathedral scene.

In *L'Etranger* the brilliance of the sun is emphasized as much as the indifference of Meursault. The burial of the mother, the murder, and the trial take place under the full glare of the hot sun. Everything shimmers in the heat haze to make the landscape inhuman and discouraging. The soil is hot red dappled with vivid green; the sundrenched countryside is so dazzling that Meursault dares not raise his eyes. On the day of the murder, the sunlight splinters into flakes of fire on the sand and the sea. On the day of the trial, the terrible heat and stuffiness of the air make Meursault a bit dizzy. Blinded and immobilized by sun and heat, Meursault in the most pregnant moments is never lucid. Unlike K., Meursault is also physically confined in a very real way by being put in prison.

There is no attempt made here to catalogue the weather reports of the city of *Der Prozess* or Algiers. What is important, however, is the emphasis that Kafka and Camus place upon not only the setting of their novels but also the particular detail of the climatic conditions in which K. and Meursault function. These conditions are specifically designed to confine the characters physically as they are limited mentally by their trials. Here, again, the authors have chosen extremes in an attempt the better to illustrate basic reality and the effect of this reality upon unrefined man.[5] The brilliance of the sun in *L'Etranger* has the same effect as the torrential rains and blinding snows of *Der Prozess*. The prison of *L'Etranger* is a realistic presentation of the confinement that K. experiences in the candlelit darkness of so many scenes of *Der Prozess*.

Correspondingly, in the final scenes of the novels, at the point that the protagonists reflect upon and realize the full impact of their trials, the weather is again in accord with the mental condition of the heroes. In the execution scene of *Der Prozess*, the moon shines on everything with that simplicity and serenity which no other light

28

possesses. And in *L'Etranger* after Meursault's interview with the priest, the stars glitter and the cool night air fans his cheeks, as he opens his heart to the benign indifference of the universe.

To enhance further the realism of the novels' setting, both authors pay painstaking care to the selection and depiction of specific detail. In novels that leave so much unsaid, these details gain in importance. Again, the novels acquire concreteness and a semblance of reality which might otherwise be lost in primarily symbolic works. What I have in mind here is that in contrast to the anonymous characters who act within the confines of the novels, the physical aspects within which they act do not remain so foreign to the reader. Somewhat paradoxically, the never-ending streets, inhabited by faceless people, have particular physical details that are immediately recognizable to anyone. Or, perhaps more to the point, it can be said that although K. and Meursault cannot see beyond their noses in respect to the conventionally observed physical attributes, they are keen observers of minutiae. Thus, when K. enters Fräulein Bürstner's room on the morning of his arrest, he sees that the night table has been pushed into the middle of the room to serve as a desk and that the inspector is rearranging a matchbox, a pincushion, and a book that lie on the table. He notices a white blouse dangling from the latch of the open window. He watches the two old creatures from across the street and observes that the third member to join their group stands squeezing and twisting his goatee with his fingers. He notices all of these things, but he fails to see the men who are in the process of deciding his fate.

In the scene with Titorelli, the same kind of description is used. Details within the studio are carefully catalogued. To K., the whole room – the floor, walls, and ceiling – is a box of bare wooden planks with cracks showing between them; the bed is covered with a variegated assortment of coverings; an easel in the middle of the room supports a canvas covered by a shirt whose sleeves dangle to the floor. K. sees every detail, yet sees nothing. Titorelli himself remains nondescript. What impression the reader has of him is gained almost exclusively from the environment in which he acts.

The same sort of observation goes on in *L'Etranger*. Meursault sees everything, yet sees nothing. He, like K., is sensitive to his surroundings, but he never projects these immediate sense impressions into any sort of relationship beyond. At his mother's wake he says of the people around him, "je les voyais comme je n'ai jamais vu personne et pas un détail de leurs visages ou de leurs habits ne m'échappait. Pourtant je ne les entendais pas et j'avais peine à croire à leur réalité" (p. 18). Here, as throughout the book, Meursault sees but cannot hear – actually and symbolically. The mortuary he sees as a bright, spotlessly clean room with whitewashed walls and a big skylight. He looks at the coffin resting on two chairs in the center of the room. The lid of the coffin is in place, but the screws have been given only a few turns and

30

their nickeled heads stick out above the dark walnut-stained wood. His recollection of the burial involves the memory of the villagers in the street, the red geraniums on the graves, Perez's fainting fit, the tawny red earth pattering on his mother's coffin, and the bits of white roots mixed up with the dirt. However, in spite of these acute observations, the observations are never projected beyond immediate sense impressions. The sentient, indifferent Meursault is the Meursault that the reader is constantly aware of on each page of the first part of the novel. As if afraid that the reader will fail to see these characteristics, Camus repeats them again and again.

Both K. and Meursault are chronic voyeurs; however the sense impression resulting from a particular detail at a given moment is the only positive effect of that detail. The detail itself is rarely retained, never studied at a future time. Consequently, the impact of the detail is recorded by both Kafka and Camus in the resultant sense reactions of the major characters. K. and Meursault are two anonymous office workers, who act within the bounds of a work-a-day world: a world somewhat limited by myopic observation, it is true, but a recognizable world full of all the distractions and all the minutiae that deter most of us from seeing any causal relationship between events, any correspondence between things. These are sentient men who are affected by and act according to the environment in which they find themselves. They are egocentrics who see nothing beyond the immediate, who do not and cannot judge their own actions. As sentients, all events are felt rather than known, and Kafka and Camus objectively report the sense impressions of their heroes. Two illustrations serve to show the technique employed by the authors.

In *Der Prozess* Kafka relates K.'s feelings in the court offices in the following words:

> Er war wie seekrank. Er glaubte auf einem Schiff zu sein, das sich in schwerem Seegang befand. Es war ihm, als stürze das Wasser gegen die Holzwände, als komme aus der Tiefe des Ganges ein Brausen her, wie von überschlagendem Wasser, als schaukle der Gang in der Quere und als würden die wartenden Parteien zu beiden Seiten gesenkt und gehoben (p. 91).

In *L'Etranger* Camus plays on the reader's senses of sight and smell as Meursault relates his impressions of the funeral procession:

> Autour de moi, c'était toujours la même campagne lumineuse gorgée de soleil. L'éclat du ciel était insoutenable. A un moment donné, nous sommes passés sur une partie de la route qui avait été récemment refaite. Le soleil avait fait éclater le goudron. Les pieds y enfonçaient et laissaient ouverte sa chair brillante. Audessus de la voiture, le chapeau du cocher, en cuir bouilli, semblait avoir été pétri dans cette boue noire. J'étais un peu perdu entre le ciel bleu et blanc et la monotonie de ces couleurs, noir

32

gluant du goudron ouvert, noir terne des habits, noir laqué de la voiture. Tout cela, le soleil, l'odeur de cuir et de crottin de la voiture, celle du vernis et celle de l'encens, la fatigue d'une nuit d'insomnie, me troublait le regard et les idées (pp. 27-28).

These two passages are perhaps unusually vivid, but they serve to clarify the point I wish to make. They are not atypical. What Kafka and Camus have done – again with the same purpose in mind – is to convey to the reader in as clear a way as possible the importance of the senses to their particular heroes. These passages gain in magnitude when the great number of the sense reactions related by the authors is compared to the almost non-existent number of passages in the first half of the novels which relate the reflective thought of K. and Meursault.

The total effect of the depictions of these sense impressions is similar in each novel, but the particular techniques vary. As can be seen in the quotations, Kafka conveys K.'s feelings metaphorically; whereas Camus conveys Meursault's impressions directly. This is a significant difference in means which does not imply a significant difference in ends. In both novels these means are but another way of emphasizing the strongly sentient aspect of K. and Meursault.

In addition to similarities in the significance of time to the protagonists, in the portrayal of characters, in the creation of settings, and in the emphasis upon sense impressions, there are other comparable techniques used by Kafka and Camus. The language and sentence structure employed by the authors and the use of counterpoint and irony also significantly add to the general appearance of reality in these works.

There is no special terminology used in either *Der Prozess* or *L'Etranger*. Both authors do everything they can to avoid abstract terms and to make their stories appear to be simple, clear-cut, everyday occurrences. Kafka's long paragraphs, which at times run on without regard for dialogue or change of pace or mood, produce much the same effect as Camus' short concise sentences.[6] Kafka's language, too, has a clipped pace and his structures are simple. In Kafka the effect is one of breathlessness, of the impatience of the modern world. In Camus the same effect is created. In his clipped sentences, each action becomes an action in and of itself that allows for no modification of past events. The action is pointed to the future and to the conclusion.[7] In both books the sentence structure creates a kind of buzzing in the reader's ear that suggests the dissonance of the modern temper.

Counterpoint is another technique used by these authors to add validity to their nightmarish creations. Corresponding to the effect of reality established by detailed description is the harassing confusion – also a very real aspect of work-a-day living – brought about by the use of counterpoint. To the melody pounded through the main themes of the chapters of their novels, Kafka and Camus

34

add a related but independent one. However, unlike musical counterpoint, the result is not a harmonic whole. It is dissonant. Again, the result is that the heroes are unable to perceive clearly what is going on. In *Der Prozess* during K.'s visit to Titorelli, the conversation and the flow of action are constantly interrupted by the activities of the girls in the hallway. During Marie's visit to Meursault in the prison, they have no privacy, no possible chance to communicate; for they are ever aware of the conversations of the other visitors and prisoners surrounding them. In these scenes, the authors give another tangible illustration of the inability of one human being to communicate with another.

The choice of everyday language and the use of counterpoint in works that have so many symbolic suggestions are ironic; but perhaps the most ironic device of all lies in the structure of the novels. In theme, in the choice of heroes, in the fate suffered by these heroes and in the heroes' attitude to their fate, these novels are analogous to Greek tragedy. In the choice of office workers as heroes, Kafka and Camus elevate the anonymous symbol of twentieth-century Western society to the role of the traditional tragic hero who faces death in order to find meaning in life,[8] and K. and Meursault are no more responsible for their actions than is such a traditionally classic hero as Oedipus.[9] Fate placed Oedipus on the road to Thebes at a particular moment in history, and fate places K. and Meursault in twentieth-century Western

35

civilization. Just as Oedipus for many years was ignorant of the monstrous lie he lived, K. and Meursault are completely unaware of the unauthenticity of the existence they adhere to. Consciousness came to Oedipus as suddenly as K. and Meursault are arrested for their crimes. The guilt of Oedipus was founded on past events, and in *Der Prozess* K.'s actions prior to his arrest, although certainly insignificantly and mechanically done at the time, suddenly take on new significance after the arrest and become the only plausible explanation for his arrest and the nightmarish trial. In Part II of *L'Etranger*, all meaningless acts of Part I gain magnitude and eventually lead to the death of Meursault. In the worlds of Oedipus, K., and Meursault, somebody performs something which is apparently quite commonplace at the time,[10] but under close examination the significance of the action gains in importance. All three figures suffer as the result of their fate, and it is at the moment of their greatest suffering that they are most noble. At the time of their deaths, K. and Meursault both discover their link of solidarity with all men – death – and it is at the time of approaching death when they perceive themselves as isolated beings and resign themselves to things which are beyond their human understanding. They die with the resignation of the classic hero, and in the fact that the shame of their deaths outlives them, they gain the stature of sacrificial figures.

These are the principal similarities in narrative

36

devices in *Der Prozess* and *L'Etranger*. There are others, such as the position of the scenes in which the protagonists reject formalized religion in the guise of the priests, but not only is the tone of the chapters sufficiently different to negate rather than to emphasize the surface similarities; however the arrangement of the chapters in *Der Prozess* was not established by Kafka.[11] The narrative devices compared in this chapter, although often difficult to define,[12] were selected to illustrate that in *Der Prozess* and *L'Etranger* these devices are used to point to, augment, and clarify the central theme of the novels: the search for meaning in life.

Much of the vitality and the beauty of these novels is dependent upon the artistic presentation of their themes. In works that emphasize man's search for meaning in a life that is limited by birth and death, the significance of time to the protagonists not only underlines the moment-to-moment philosophy of K. and Meursault, but also beats a rhythmic reminder into the reader's ear that all life is measured in moments. By the time the reader has progressed to the chapter "Im Dom" and to Part II of *L'Etranger*, he has become so caught up in the momentum of the time flow that the stopping of it has the same effect as the arrival of the eleventh hour in a horror film. The reader perceives, almost subconsciously, that something important is about to take place. It is precisely so, for it is in these sections of the novels that Kafka and Camus fully develop their philosophy. The authors' particular use of time is the most important single device in *Der Prozess* and *L'Etranger;* for once the major characters are set within a framework of time, the portrayal of these characters and their reactions to the things about them is semi-dictated. K. and Meursault cannot be men who philosophize about the meaning of life and seek to relate the future to the present and the present to the past. Time rushes them from second to second, and they can only perceive fleetingly the people and the events that they brush by. It is therefore the sense rather than the intellectual perception of K. and Meursault that is emphasized. Until time is stopped, these men feel their way through life in a pathetic, bungling and yet amazing way. Thus, Kafka and Camus, through an extremely effective manipulation of K. and Meursault, seem to tell their readers that life is like this unless one is fully conscious of its absurdity and acts in every moment with the complete awareness that it may well be the last.

With one important distinction, *Der Prozess* and
L'Etranger have many qualities in common with
murder mysteries. The world is disquieting, the
mood is uncanny, the scene is drenched in either
candle and moonlight or blinding sun, but in these
novels the guilty remain free and the innocent are
executed. Joseph K. commits no specified crime
and the killing of the Arab has little or nothing to
do with Meursault's conviction; yet both K. and
Meursault are sentenced to death. It is a disquieting world, indeed, that permits men to die like
dogs and be executed for smoking at a wake. It is
a strange world, but not a foreign one. By allowing
such acts to take place, Kafka and Camus skillfully
criticize a contemporary society in which false
values triumph and real values lose. In these
novels society is played against the individual at
every turn, and by mere strength of numbers is
victorious. What Kafka and Camus have done is
to prove guilt in reverse fashion. Through the
executions of K. and Meursault, they accuse the
false social structure that brought about these
deaths, and simultaneously plead the cause of the
individual whose individuality is squelched by the
unauthenticity of society. The trials, then, are
actually contests between the coexisting forces of
authentic and unauthentic existence, and each
character and action in the books is carefully
maneuvered to highlight this duality.

In *Der Prozess* the reader is first aware of this
duality at the point of arrest. The fact that Franz
and Willem proceed to arrest K. in Fräulein

p. 51

Bürstner's room and not his own is no chance happening. This act is the first of many attempts to transplant K. from his unreal world into a world that in all its strangeness is his real existence. As René Dauvin says, "Joseph K. had lived in bad faith; obliged to choose between two existential possibilities, he had chosen unauthentic existence and betrayed what was deepest and most personal in him for the benefit of a superficial and reassuring way of life."[1] K. could not be arrested in his own room, for his room was a part of the unauthentic world he chose to live in. By transferring him to the room next door, he is removed from his immediate surroundings into an environment that is foreign and yet close to him. This environment is carefully populated by enough people with whom K. is familiar to divorce it from the fantastic; and at the same time, faces and objects that are unfamiliar to K. suffice to jar him out of any feeling of complacency.

Up to the point of his arrest, Joseph K. was a man similar to other men, but on the day of the arrest, the security of routine is cancelled for him; and from this moment until his death, he oscillates between the worlds of real and of false values. At every turn he is invited to put aside the dictates of society and to enter into his own individuality, but he can never completely free himself from the practical, secure world he had once known in order to face the chaotic world that is his own. He constantly searches for a logical solution to his trial and there is none. His failure to realize that his

40

trial is personal and to take his total self into account is the ultimate cause of his death. He must die because he will not leave the unauthentic world.

The action of *Der Prozess* constantly alternates from the world of real values to the world of false values. Kafka very skillfully uses the characters that K. contacts during the action of the trial to convey these changes. After his arrest, the first person with whom K. converses at any length is his landlady, Frau Grubach. Of the arrest, she says, "Es handelt sich ja um Ihr Glück." And later, "... aber diese Verhaftung. – Es kommt mir wie etwas Gelehrtes vor ... es kommt mir wie etwas Gelehrtes vor, das ich zwar nicht verstehe, das man aber auch nicht verstehen muss" (p. 30). K.'s reply to her is that "... ich ... halte es einfach nicht einmal für etwas Gelehrtes, sondern überhaupt für nichts ... hätte ich vernünftig gehandelt, so wäre nichts weiter geschehen ... Man ist aber so wenig vorbereitet. In der Bank ... bin ich vorbereitet" (pp. 30-31). The contrast between the two worlds is beautifully illustrated in this brief encounter. Frau Grubach's interpretation of the arrest is based solely upon feeling. K., unable to perceive through instinct, attempts to explain away the entire episode in rational terminology. He blames the arrest upon his unpreparedness, and his idea of being prepared involves material things exterior to himself: the general telephone, the office phone, clients and clerks. He fails to see that at the bank he is completely submerged in practi-

41

calities which are artificial aids to cover his basic insecurity.[2]

K. next speaks with Fräulein Bürstner. In trying to free himself from his anxiety, he tells her of the arrest. Perhaps he hopes to discover in the re-enactment of the morning's happenings some logical explanation of the proceedings. But his attempt fails. He not only gains no explanation, but he also estranges the possible friendship of Fräulein Bürstner. She is indifferent to him and to the arrest. To people of her world, such things as an inexplicable arrest do not occur. Furthermore, she is a woman, and like Leni and the bailiff's wife, Fräulein Bürstner symbolizes tendencies that cannot be reduced to the rational.

The law court is the clearest presentation of the world of authentic existence. In a court that sits only at night and on Sundays in crowded, stuffy attics, K. comes into immediate contact with the realm of real values. This is the world of being, completely divorced from material appearance. Here it does not matter if one is a house painter or a junior manager of a large bank; here the law books studied deal with aspects of life labeled as indecent by organized society.[3] K., however, sees none of this. He is incapable of giving up the material world and penetrating into the world of feeling. From a materialistic viewpoint, all that K. can see is the external appearance of the court. And that repulses him in the same way that the raw life of the tenement district in which the court is situated repulses him. For K., only appearance is important.

After his initial contact with the court, K. returns to the world of unauthentic existence. It is at this point that his Uncle Karl induces him to consult a lawyer. The uncle is a man of action and, as such, sees in K.'s trial a threat not only to K. but to the entire family and to the social-economic structure upon which society is built. Uncle Karl contacts K. in the bank, the place where K. would be most vulnerable to the seemingly logical suggestion of contacting a lawyer, and after some discussion, the two drive to the lawyer Huld.

Huld is another representative of the finite and foreseeable world. In antithesis to the men of the court, Huld personifies abstract reason, which in this particular case attempts to solve without even questioning. The lawyer is, of course, powerless to suggest any solution to a case that is strictly personal. "The light which the lawyer sheds on the affair is as pale as the light of his candle."[4]

Disgusted with the lack of progress made with his case by Huld, K. turns from abstract reason and attempts to find an answer to his enigma in art. Titorelli, the artist, represents the world of appearance. Kafka tells that he is called Titorelli, but that this is only his pseudonym. His real name is unknown. This detail strengthens the idea that since art deals in illusion it cannot be a part of authentic existence. The unreality of the world of appearance is symbolized by the use of the pseudonym Titorelli in the same way that the inadequacy of the world of pure intellect is symbolized by the dim candlelight of Huld's chamber. The most that Titorelli can offer K. is ostensible acquittal or postponement; neither gives K. any hope for freedom.[5]

Following his contact with Titorelli, K. dismisses the advocate Huld. It is at this point that K. becomes completely immersed in his trial. Nothing else has any meaning to him. K. has exhausted every means at his disposal in the attempt to find a solution to his trial, but he is still totally unaware that it is a personal affair and cannot be solved by any agency exterior to himself. At the time of his deepest despair, K. is asked to accompany an Italian visitor to the bank on a tour of the cathedral. After seeking an answer to his case in the rational world and the world of appearance, this is K.'s first contact with the religious world.

Religion also proffers no answer. Although the explanation of K.'s failure lies in the legend of the doorkeeper as told by the priest, formalized religion has nothing to do with this explanation. When K. enters the cathedral square, it is completely deserted. Within the cathedral, the only people are an old woman muffled in a shawl and a limping verger. K. himself goes to the cathedral with a guide book rather than a prayer book. The cathedral is so dark that K. must use a flashlight to look at the paintings, and the one painting that he examines is a portrayal of Christ being laid in the tomb. All of these details emphatically illustrate the idea that for contemporary man,

44

God is dead.[6] Again K. is being told that man is totally responsible for all his actions and must call upon and question himself in order to find a meaning to his life. He cannot ignore self, for by so doing he belies his first responsibility to life.

As seen in the light of man's total responsibility, the legend of the doorkeeper has a specific meaning. Since K. stumbled upon this explanation by chance (as a guide for the Italian) and not through inner questioning, it can be only an explanation of life and not a way to freedom for K. K. must die like a dog, for he has not attained the status of a complete human being.[7] The priest says to K., "Du suchst zuviel fremde Hilfe ..." (p. 253). K. has been deluded by false values during the course of his trial, and his particular delusion is explained by the legend.

Since the legend incorporates the specific meaning of the trial, it warrants close analysis. It begins:

Vor dem Gesetz [law to Kafka is "that which is indestructible and to believe is to free the indestructible in oneself, to be indestructible, or more exactly, to be"] steht ein Türhüter [the block between man and himself: parents, religion, society – the world]. Zu diesem Türhüter kommt ein Mann [K., everyman] vom Lande [innocent of social complexities; perhaps from childhood where all is accepted at face value and nothing is inexplicable] und bittet um Eintritt in das Gesetz. Aber der Türhüter sagt, dass er ihm jetzt den Eintritt nicht gewähren könne [the *er* is important here; only the "I" can grant itself entrance to the law. The man, as K., has been awakened to the awareness of law, but, also as K., has only reached the brink of understanding. His own inadequacies keep him from attainment of final understanding]. Der Mann überlegt und fragt dann, ob er also später werde eintreten dürfen. "Es ist möglich" sagt der Türhüter, "jetzt aber nicht". [For the man the possibility of knowing is sufficient to justify his eternal quest, and for the doorkeeper the possibility exists if the man turns toward and questions himself.] Da das Tor zum Gesetz offensteht wie immer [the possibility is always open] und der Türhüter beiseite tritt [invitation] bückt sich der Mann [curiosity] um durch das Tor Innere zu sehen. Als der Türhüter das merkt, lacht er und sagt: "Wenn es dich so lockt, versuche es doch, trotz meinem Verbot hineinzugehen. Merke aber: Ich bin mächtig. Und ich bin nur der unterste Türhüter. Von Saal zu Saal stehen aber Türhüter, einer mächtiger als der andere. Schon den Anblick des dritten kann nicht einmal ich mehr vertragen." [To face oneself is difficult, and as man begins to break down the superfluities surrounding himself, the aspect of the real becomes increasingly unbearable.] Solche Schwierigkeiten hat der Mann vom Lande nicht erwartet, das Gesetz soll doch jedem und immer zugänglich sein, denkt er, aber als er jetzt den Türhüter in seinem Pelzmantel genauer ansieht, seine grosse

46

Spitznase, den langen, dünnen, schwarzen,
tartarischen Bart, entschliesst er sich doch,
lieber zu warten, bis er die Erlaubnis zum
Eintritt bekommt. [On the brink of understanding, it is easier to resign than to surmount
the immediate obstacle. This situation parallels
K.'s reaction to his first contact with the court.]
Der Türhüter gibt ihm einen Schemel [comfort]
und lässt ihn seitwärts von der Tür sich nieder-
setzen. Dort sitzt er [passivity] Tage und Jahre
[once aware of the possibility of communion
with the law there is no escape back to innocence.] Er macht viele Versuche eingelassen zu
werden und ermüdet den Türhüter durch seine
Bitten. [As K. attempted to attain admittance
to the court through the advocate and the
artist.] Der Türhüter stellt öfters kleine Verhöre
mit ihm an, fragt ihn nach seiner Heimat aus
und nach vielem anderen, es sind aber teil-
nahmslose Fragen, wie sie grosse Herren stellen,
und zum Schlusse sagt er ihm immer wieder,
dass er ihn noch nicht einlassen könne. [Rein-
forcement of the idea that the guard (anyone
outside of self) is unable to grant admission to
the law.] Der Mann, der sich für seine Reise mit
vielem ausgerüstet hat, verwendet alles, und sei
es noch so wertvoll, um den Türhüter zu be-
stechen. [K. abandons his position, his educa-
tion, his sense of values, everything but himself
in order to be free of his trial.] Dieser nimmt
zwar alles an, aber sagt dabei: "Ich nehme es
nur an, damit du nicht glaubst, etwas versäumt

zu haben." [Again the cold indifference to the burning quest.] Während der vielen Jahre beobachtet der Mann den Türhüter fast ununterbrochen. Er vergisst die anderen Türhüter, und dieser erst scheint ihm das einzige Hindernis für den Eintritt in das Gesetz. [All foresight is lost; he is only aware of the immediate hindrance.] Er verflucht den unglücklichen Zufall in den ersten Jahren laut, später, als er alt wird, brummt er nur noch vor sich hin. Er wird kindisch, und da er in dem jahrelangen Studium des Türhüters auch die Flöhe in seinem Pelzkragen erkannt hat, bittet er auch die Flöhe, ihm zu helfen und den Türhüter umzustimmen. [K., too, in the beginning cursed his fate, struggled to maintain his equilibrium, and finally succumbed to his trial. K., also, consulted the filth connected with the court (the fleas) before his final resignation.] Schliesslich wird sein Augenlicht schwach, und er weiss nicht, ob es um ihn wirklich dunkler wird oder ob ihn nur die Augen täuschen. [Complete withdrawal from the world of reality causes his rational faculties to fail; he doubts his own judgment.] Wohl aber erkennt er jetzt im Dunkel einen Glanz, der unverlöschlich aus der Türe des Gesetzes bricht. [The light of the law becomes brighter as he approaches its meaning. To perceive this light does not depend on one's ability to see the world around him.] Nun lebt er nicht mehr lange. Vor seinem Tode sammeln sich in seinem Kopfe alle Erfahrungen der ganzen

48

Zeit zu einer Frage, die er bisher an den Türhüter noch nicht gestellt hat. Er winkt ihm zu, da er seinen erstarrenden Körper nicht mehr aufrichten kann. Der Türhüter muss sich tief zu ihm hinunterneigen, denn die Grössenunterschiede haben sich sehr zuungunsten des Mannes verändert. "Was willst du denn jetzt noch wissen?" fragt der Türhüter. "Du bist unersättlich." "Alle streben doch nach dem Gesetz", sagt der Mann, "wie kommt es, dass in den vielen Jahren niemand ausser mir Einlass verlangt hat?" Der Türhüter erkennt, dass der Mann schon am Ende ist, und um sein vergehendes Gehör noch zu erreichen, brüllt er ihn an "Hier konnte niemand sonst Einlass erhalten, denn dieser Eingang war nur für dich bestimmt. Ich gehe jetzt und schliesse ihn." [Death comes to the lonely man as it comes to the lonely K. Both become aware of the most obvious question only after they have squandered their lives. The bellowing of the doorkeeper mocks their failure, and they die "wie ein Hund." There can be no understanding of the law by the man who refuses to question himself; admission to the law does not come after life; man either attains understanding of the law in this life or the door to understanding is locked forever.][8]

Der Prozess ends in failure. The novel opens with Joseph K.'s subjection to an arrest which he constantly questions but never understands. In his frantic pursuit of release from this trial, he loses all sense of proportion. K. was awakened from an inactive, unproductive, habitual existence. He was to break from this inactivity and enter into the excitement of an active life. Failing to see the potentialities in his own life and failing to share his own with his fellow men, he merely substitutes a new monster for the old. He pursues his trial; he allows his trial to become a part of himself; and he is again doomed to failure. He meets each situation materialistically and learns nothing about himself. He receives neither help nor encouragement, not because other men are unwilling to help but because they cannot. They cannot know K., for K. refuses to know himself. The trial is insignificant to them, for the trial is personal. The trial is ridiculous to them because they have either surmounted their own trials and become members of the court, or they have never been a part of the impersonal world. In either case they belong to a common group. Symbolically that which they have in common is their humanity – their oneness with the species. K. dies like a dog and not like a man, for he had never attained the right to die like a man.[9] He failed to question himself and then project his being into the community of man.

Joseph K.'s failure to recognize that his anxiety was caused by his inability to question himself is certainly a result of his own inadequacies as a man, but more than these inadequacies, the exterior social trappings in which he was submerged kept him from seeing the real nature of life. Society,

50

according to Kafka, has no category for the independent man, and the anguish felt by man is a direct consequence of mass pressures. Contemporary man is at home nowhere. He may seek to be independent, but at the same moment he wishes social approval.[10] In *Der Prozess* society has been found guilty of K.'s murder. Society has killed the peculiarities, man is dead. What Kafka implies is that to be an individual in contemporary civilization is to be a stranger.

If Kafka had created a character who descended out of the darkness of the night into the clarity of the dawn, that character might be Camus' Meursault.[11] As K., Meursault is also a victim of contemporary society; however, unlike K., Meursault triumphs over social pressures and dies not in resignation to but in defiance of all that brought about his destruction.[12]

In *L'Etranger* Camus juxtaposes the worlds of authentic and unauthentic existence, and like Kafka's, Camus' characters illustrate these two worlds in action. The reader is first aware of this division at the time of Meursault's arrest. Up to the moment of the murder, no moral judgment of Meursault's actions was necessary; however, the murder upsets the careful balance maintained by the social order, and society under the guise of the law must intervene to re-establish that order.

Throughout the first section of the book, Meursault is depicted as a man whose actions are based entirely on sense impressions. He is not a *révolté* who is conscious of the absurdity of life, nor is he a totally indifferent man. Meursault lives for the moment and every moment is of equal value to him; but in contrast to a completely indifferent man, each act is not of equal magnitude. He is an office worker in Algiers and his life is a life of seeming indifference. For example, it makes no difference if he marries Marie or not, or if Céleste is a man much more worthy of his friendship than Raymond, or if he is transferred to a Parisian office or remains at Algiers. These ordinarily important judgments are inconsequential to him, but the sense impressions of the dry roller towel in the washroom at midday or the changing aspects of the sky or the smell of brine in Marie's hair saturate his existence. He lives in a world foreign to socially accepted values; the everyday questions which torment the average individual have no meaning to Meursault. He questions nothing.

Marie at one time when she is discussing marriage with Meursault murmurs something about his being a queer fellow, but at no other time in the first section of the book does anyone pass judgment upon anyone else. Marie, Raymond, Salamano, Masson are of one world with Meursault. They accept each moment for what it is and never question the reason behind any action. In the first part of the book, Meursault's indifference is mentioned over and over. He is sure of nothing and cares about nothing that leads to any rational judgment.

This world of rational indifference is not the world of real values, but the people of this world are the people who can gain authentic existence; for they are outside of the social barriers that ordinarily bar man from becoming aware of his human condition. In the first part of *L'Etranger* these people exist free from society but unauthentically. Their sin is that they question nothing.[13] It is equal to K.'s sin of insatiability; to Meursault no act is consequential; to K. no act is inconsequential. Neither faces himself.

In Part II of *L'Etranger*, Meursault undergoes a change from the purely sentient to a conscious man in revolt. His thought develops from matter-of-fact acceptance to that of a man who is fully conscious of the absurdity of life and impassioned with the desire to live "sans abdiquer aucune de ces certitudes, sans lendemain, sans espoir, sans illusions, sans résignation non plus."[14] The change is gradual and it is not until the last page of the book that he realizes that "le présent et la succession des présents devant une âme sans cesse consciente, c'est l'idéal de l'homme absurde."[15]

At the beginning of his imprisonment, Meursault gradually learns to accept his position in much the same way that as an office worker he accepted his eight-hour work day. At first he finds it difficult to remember that he is not a free man, but soon the things he used to care for: women, the ocean, cigarettes – become trivial and no longer occupy his mind. He returns to the thought that "on finissait par s'habituer à tout" (p. 110). He sleeps sixteen to eighteen hours a day and only six hours remain for him to kill "avec les repas, les

53

besoins naturels, mes souvenirs et l'histoire du Tchécoslovaque" (p. 113). Meursault remains the unthinking man who, rather than questioning, adjusts to a situation; however, these worlds of memory, sleep and solitude to which he adjusts are new to Meursault and are responsible for his eventual development in character.

Even in the early phases of his imprisonment, certain alterations in his character are perceptible. When the guard explains to Meursault the reason for the deprivation of women and cigarettes which a prisoner must suffer, Meursault is provoked to thought. Up to this moment, he had never bothered to think: liberty or the lack of it had no meaning to him. From this first awareness, follows a succession of thoughts directed to himself and to the meaning of life. He begins to remember and remarks. "J'ai compris alors qu'un homme qui n'aurait vécu qu'un seul jour pourrait sans peine vivre cent ans dans une prison" (p. 113). He passes his first judgment when he says of the story about the Czech who had been murdered by his mother, "... je trouvais que le voyageur l'avait un peu mérité et qu'il ne faut jamais jouer" (p. 114).

The actual trial is a succession of firsts for Meursault: "... pour la première fois ... j'ai senti combien j'étais déstesté par tous ces gens-là" (p. 127); "pour la première fois, j'ai compris que j'étais coupable" (p. 128); "c'est la première fois de ma vie que j'ai eu envie d'embrasser un homme" (p. 132). After the end of the day's proceedings, after Meursault is again in his cell, he says,

54

"Comme si les chemins familiers tracés dans les ciels d'été pouvaient mener aussi bien aux prisons qu'aux sommeils innocents" (p. 138). These thoughts are in direct contrast to the indifferent statements uttered by Meursault in the first part of the book. To realize, to understand, to want, to learn are all new experiences for Meursault. The gradual change that takes place in his way of thinking brings him closer to his understanding of life and to his eventual revolt against it. The alteration in character is brought about by his contact with the world of unauthentic values.

From the time of his arrest, Meursault is forced to enter a world peopled by men foreign to his understanding. Marie, Raymond, Céleste, Salamano, Masson never looked upon Meursault as being strange; his actions were never questioned by them. Until his imprisonment, the only contact Meursault had with people unlike himself was through observation. He sensed that the men and women at his mother's funeral, that the lady automaton, that his boss had a set of values different from his; however, as is typical of Meursault, he never questioned what these values were. At best he observed these characters. Of the inhabitants of the old folk's home he says, "Je les voyais comme je n'ai jamais vu personne et pas un détail de leurs visages ou de leurs habits ne m'échappait" (p. 18). The little robot-woman Meursault sees as "une bizarre petite femme, qui ... avait des gestes saccades et des yeux brillants dans une petite figure de pomme" (p. 66). He does not describe his boss, but from the words, "Il ... m'a dit que je répondais toujours à côté, que je n'avais pas d'ambition ..." (p. 64) it is clear that the boss, too, had values different from Meursault's. His mother's friends, the robot-woman, and his boss bring Meursault into contact with representatives of different values, but not until he is imprisoned does the meaning of these values have any direct effect upon him. After his arrest these are the men who try him, and Meursault must deal with them. It is from his being forced to do more than merely observe these people that Meursault finally evaluates their thoughts and through questioning of himself, not feeling, dismisses them as representatives of false values.

In prison his first contact with unreal values is the law. This is the law of social order that eventually tries and convicts Meursault for his previous life of indifference. By firing the shots into the Arab, Meursault had upset the social order and society had to sit in judgment upon him. This much Meursault understands, but the law as it is depicted in *L'Etranger* is not so clear-cut or honest. In the initial scene with the lawyer, it is obvious that Meursault as a personality is on trial. The first thing that the lawyer talked about to him was the great callousness that he had shown at his mother's funeral. When Meursault remarked that his mother's death had no connection with the charge against him, the lawyer replied that this answer indicated that Meursault had never had any dealings with the law. This scene is immediately

56

followed by the questioning on the part of the magistrate. Again, it is clear that Meursault is on trial because he is a threat to all that organized society holds dear. Before the magistrate, Meursault refuses to repent his crime, and when asked if he believes in God, he simply replies, "No." To the magistrate this denial of God is unthinkable; never before in all his experience had a prisoner not wept when he saw the crucifix.

In the beginning stages of his trial, Meursault has brought into question two of the most sacred tenets of organized society: motherhood and God. In his inability to become overtly emotional about either, Meursault has committed his greatest sins. To the unauthentic world, lip service to certain values suffices; the question of sincerity is never raised. Meursault in his refusal to give this lip service is seen as a threat to the status quo.[16] If the sanctity of motherhood and God is allowed to be questioned, two social strongholds collapse. Here, as in *Der Prozess*, the logic of the law is ill-equipped to handle any situation outside the accepted limits. As is true for K., the trial from the initial contact with legal mechanics becomes an increasingly personal trial for Meursault. According to Kafka and Camus, the legal machinery is faulty and a society which conforms to certain codes in order to cover up the incomprehensibility of life is a superficial and guilty order.

Having illustrated the inadequacies of legal codes to answer man's trial, Camus next brings Meursault into contact with organized religion.

The supernatural aspects of religion are as inadequate as the rational concepts of the law. After the trial the prison chaplain comes to speak to Meursault about forgiveness and an after-life in which all sinners may be redeemed. These ideas have no meaning to a man who is sure of his present life and of the death that is coming. For the first time, Meursault breaks out into violent rage and his thoughts formulate. He denies after-life. The only life that he recognizes is life as he knew it with the sea and the sun and the softness of Marie's body. The death of others, a mother's love, God make no difference to him. All men must die one day, and it does not matter to him if he is executed for not weeping at his mother's funeral. In the final analysis, it is all the same. The only difference between him and other men is that he knows both the glory of life and the unjustifiable nature of death. After this outburst, Meursault is calm for the first time since his imprisonment. He is no longer tormented by hope, for now he realizes that life is void of hope. He accepts the inevitability of his death, but more than that, for the first time Meursault is an aware individual. The questions that had been teeming within him since his arrest – perhaps even before[17] – are asked and answered. Meursault affirms for the first time. He denies the world of false values and searches within himself and finds the real meaning of life.

As an aware individual sentenced to death, Meursault becomes a sacrificial character. On the

58

eve of his execution, Meurault finds the nature of authentic existence. He learns that life is absurd because man must die, and that if man is to derive full value from life, he must live it moment-by-moment, painfully conscious of its transitoriness. Aware that his death binds him to all other men, Meursault is able to go happily to his execution.[18] Meursault, unlike K., has recognized that the trials that man undergoes are his personal trials which can be absolved only through inner questioning and not by a false social structure which keeps man from facing the question of his fate and his destiny. Thus Meursault may desire cries of hatred from the crowd at his execution, for in these cries will be a sign that the spectators have abandoned all the myths which mask their human fate and recognize in him a symbol of their fate;[19] whereas K. must face his execution alone and die like a dog.

Through the trials of the two fictional characters K. and Meursault, Kafka and Camus have presented the same philosophical point of view. The guilt of both K. and Meursault is established by the lives they led prior to their trials rather than by any specific crimes that they committed. But the guilt is not theirs alone. K. and Meursault, as representatives of man in contemporary society, were forced to overcome almost insurmountable obstacles. Society under the guise of the family, the law, the church has originated codes by which modern man is expected to conduct his life. Any deviation from these codes is looked upon suspiciously. There is no place in the social set-up for the individual who attempts to go beyond or to ignore these superimposed barriers. Consequently, if K. does not turn inwardly to himself and question the meaning of life, the fault is only partially his. Raised in a social milieu that automatically turned to the law with rational questions and to the church with irrational ones, K. could be expected to do little else. He was conditioned to live in the security of the average man and to question nothing. To penetrate into the region of feeling, K. would have to have been able to give up everything materialistic, but he understood none of this. According to the judgment placed upon him, he had to rediscover the meaning of the human condition, but it was impossible for him to do that. He turned to law and to the world of day-by-day existence and at each turn he found confusion. He could not find himself. The only way out of his anxiety was to succumb to the murder by the two assistants; suicide would have given meaning to his life, and K. never found that meaning.[20] With failing eyes K. watched his own execution and said, "Wie ein Hund!" as if he meant the shame to outlive him. He wanted to go on living, he wanted to penetrate the meaning of his trial, but K. was an inadequate human being – a product of unauthentic society.

In *L'Etranger* Meursault progresses one point beyond K. He, too, is tried and convicted by a society steeped in false values, but unlike K., Meursault becomes an aware individual. Meursault was confined[21] and in his confinement he was forced to deal with issues that K. in his groping about was never aware of. Meursault had to give up the material world and to turn his questioning inwardly. If he wished to free himself from doubt and uncertainty, he alone could be the agent of that freedom. Meursault, too, was forced to deal with a contradictory world before he found the strength of his own self. He, too, had to be examined by and examine the legal and religious worlds before he could find any meaning to human life. He had to admit to himself that the simplest lives led could not be successful if the total being were not taken into question. The life of the bookkeeper who questioned nothing was not a genuine life. To be, one had to question and one had to question himself. This was the great lesson learned by Meursault.

That Meursault succeeded and K. failed in solving his enigma does not negate the fact that in either case it is society which has brought man to his dilemma. It is society that forced these men into lives of resignation and revolt. Society in its attempt to organize the world on an impersonal basis has killed God and the individual. Man is a wreck, adrift in a world devoid of meaning. The only hope left for him is to turn toward himself and to rediscover the reason for his being and a meaning in life. Kafka and Camus place the total guilt on society, and in the martyrdom of K. and Meursault they offer a possible way for mankind to surmount its trial.

Although it is difficult to speak of symbols in works whose outstanding characteristic is their apparent naturalness, it is precisely in the interpretation of the symbols that the underlying meaning of *Der Prozess* and *L'Etranger* is discernible. As has been seen, the language of the novels tends to be realistic, the characters and settings are drawn from the world of our experience, and the action of the novels is direct. The naturalness of these books, however, is derived from the characters' acceptance of what happens to them rather than from the naturalness of the events themselves. That a man should be arrested, yet totally free; or that he should be tried for matricide and parricide when in reality he murdered an Arab are illogical acts, but the reader accepts these absurd actions as natural everyday happenings because neither K. nor Meursault questions them. It is only after rereading the novels that the reader is aware of a symbolic meaning underlying all the events.

Throughout the entire works ordinary details carry meaning beyond their immediate significance. For example, it is not by chance that the warders insist that Joseph K. wear a black coat the morning of his arrest. The black is symbolic of his coming death, and K. understands its symbolism; for he says, "'Es ist doch noch nicht die Hauptverhandlung.' Die Wächter lächelten, blieben aber bei ihrem: 'Es muss ein schwarzer Rock sein'" (p. 18). Black as a symbol of death is also used in the opening pages of *L'Etranger*. Meursault

62

says, "J'étais un peu étourdi parce qu'il a fallu que je monte chez Emmanuel pour lui emprunter une cravate noire et un brassard" (p. 10). If one recalls that Emmanuel was the name given by Isaiah to the Messiah of his prophecy, the meaning of the selected detail becomes quite clear.

Although it would be wrong to attempt to interpret everything in detail,[1] an interpretation of the major symbols used by Kafka and Camus can do much to clarify the central themes of these works. The all-encompassing symbol of each novel is embedded in its title. *Der Prozess* and *L'Etranger* are words chosen to symbolize the struggle of an individual within a society foreign to his understanding. In the discussion of the techniques and the point of view employed by Kafka and Camus, many of the individual symbols used in these works have been clarified. What remains to be done is to discern the major symbols and to illustrate how these symbols are employed to enhance the meaning of the novels. We have seen that K. and Meursault are men pitted against a basically hostile world, a world that offers no way out. They, as individuals, are kept from a clear insight into the real nature of things by the superimposed structures of a false society. They oscillate between the worlds of authentic and unauthentic existence and try to govern their lives according to two contradictory sets of rules: one for the practical and social world and the other for the exercise of their own intelligence. Any such endeavor is doomed to fail; and the purpose of

Der Prozess and *L'Etranger* seems to be to point out this false dichotomy.

The struggle of K. and Meursault to be individuals in a thoroughly collective society is realistically presented in their contacts with the authoritarian aspects of civil and clerical law. This same battle is waged on a symbolic level among the main characters of the books and the natural forces which control their environment. In *Der Prozess* and *L'Etranger* the central action involves a trinity of characters which is representative of the father, the mother, and the son. A link between the philosophical and psychological viewpoints is found in the authors' use of natural symbols. In *Der Prozess* light and dark, air and airlessness; and in *L'Etranger* the sun and the sea are clearly associated with the mother and father images.

Any one familiar with the writings of Kafka knows the significance for him of his life-long struggle with his father. Although it is wrong to interpret Kafka's writings solely as a manifestation of his personal problem, the misunderstanding between the father and the son is reflected in almost all of his works. In *Der Prozess* the conflict is with the group father rather than with one set father image. Here the father browbeats the son in terms of the social code.

K.'s initial contact with the father occurs in the chapter entitled "Erste Untersuchung." The examining magistrate represents the father as an authoritarian. The conversation between K. and the

64

magistrate has many of the qualities common to
any argument between a father and a son. When
K. arrives at the court, the magistrate-father
draws out his watch and says, "Sie hätten vor
einer Stunde und fünf Minuten erscheinen sollen"
(p. 52). K. defends his tardiness in an obviously
childish way, "Mag ich zu spät gekommen sein,
jetzt bin ich hier" (p. 53). The magistrate retorts,
"Ja ... aber ich bin nicht mehr verpflichtet, Sie
jetzt zu verhören ... ich will es jedoch aus-
nahmsweise heute noch tun. Eine solche Ver-
spätung darf sich aber nicht mehr wiederholen"
(p. 53). K. then proceeds to perform for the father
image, and in a bombastic, egocentric tirade, he
attempts to belittle the magistrate and all the
years of experience that his age represents. The
magistrate permits K. to state his opinion but
obviously pays no attention to his arguments, for
at the end of the hearing he says, "Ich wollte
Sie nur darauf aufmerksam machen ... dass Sie
sich heute ... des Vorteils beraubt haben, den ein
Verhör für den Verhafteten in jedem Falle be-
deutet" (p. 63). No detailed analysis is necessary
to recognize the characteristics of this discussion.
The father insists upon his rights as an authority;
and the son, although put out by what he calls
sheer nonsense, is, all the same, impressed by what
the father has to say.

In contrast to the dogmatic father who demands
and attains K.'s respect, Uncle Karl is symbolic of
the father as Babbitt. He is a man of practical
affairs who in his bellowing, sputtering way

frequently embarrasses K. In K.'s office the uncle talks so loudly that K. has to ask him to quiet down. Later when the uncle curses Leni, K. rushes over to him with the intention of clapping both hands over his mouth. His loud laughter before the chief clerk of the court further embarrasses K. Uncle Karl is the father as a vulgar bourgeois. His vulgarity is illustrated by his brashness, and the conversation between K. and him indicates his middle-class ethics. His speech is saturated with trite phraseology. Such statements as "Josef, lieber Josef, denke an dich, an deine Verwandten, an unsern guten Namen!" (p. 116), or "... was soll denn daraus werden!" (p. 117), or "Du weisst, dass ich für dich alles tue" (p. 118) are all time-worn pleas employed by the middle class father to force his son back into the socially accepted behavior pattern. To this type of father, the opinion of society is infinitely more important than any single personal problem. Karl has no real concern for K. He impresses upon K. his connections with certain influential people who might be able to help tackle the whole nasty affair before it has had a chance to threaten the family position, but the effect or the meaning of the trial to K. is of no significance to this practical, business-like father.

K.'s contact with Huld, Titorelli and the priest brings him into association with the father as a proponent of a particular kind of knowledge. The lawyer Huld gives K. professional advice on a strictly rational, impersonal basis. He is full of

meaningless prattle and actually gets nowhere. He
tells K. about the court and his personal relations
with the officials there. He boasts of his connections with the officials, but he in reality does
nothing. His only function is to supply information, for his impersonality keeps him from ever
asking a question. The artist Titorelli, on the
other hand, questions K., and he, too, can only
inform. With the artist-father dealing in the finite
rather than the abstract world, K. momentarily
finds some hope of attaining a solution to his
problem. In the portraits of the court officials, K.
sees the possibility of limiting the incomprehensible. Here, the father is able to get the son into a
defined relationship with his problem, but the
relationship cannot be valid, for it is based upon
appearance rather than fact. The portraits of the
officials are total invention. The painter is told
what to paint and he paints it. Titorelli can do no
more then explain to K. what appears to be the
situation in respect to his trial. No more satis-
factory is the answer proffered by the priest. Here
the father gives the son information in the form of
example. He makes no claims upon the son but
seeks to inform him through the parable of the
doorkeeper. Again, the father remains aloof to the
son and openly expresses his thought that he must
speak to him from a distance so as not to be
influenced or to forget his duty. As in the case
of Huld and of Titorelli, the priest also offers K. a
form of knowledge. That none judges or sympa-

thizes is characteristic of a father's relationship with an "unclean" son.

Captain Lanz and the Whipper are representative of the father in two other roles. Captain Lanz is the father as a normal sexual male, the father as a lover. As such the son has no communication with him. K. observes Captain Lanz in his dealings with Fräulein Montag and he speaks of him often, but there is no verbal contact between the two of them. In the case of the Whipper, K. is forced to accept the total responsibility of his actions. The Whipper is symbolic of the father's role as punisher. No matter how the son pleads, there is no possible way to alleviate the punishment. Although the punishment is not physically inflicted upon K., it is a result of his actions and consequently his.

The understanding of K.'s strugggle as a battle against a group father symbol is essential to the understanding of *Der Prozess*. In the argument that K. is an individual attempting to find some meaning in life and constantly being frustrated by exterior forces, these forces seen as a father image clarify the larger scope of the argument. On a strictly personal level, Kafka has reinforced the universal aspect of his book. He has expanded a common psychological experience into one whose validity could be questioned on a universal plane. As he projects K. into everyman, he expands the father-son relationship into the man-world relationship. Seen in its more limited perspective, the argument gains credibility, and from the ac-

68

ceptance of the validity of the symbolic level, the acknowledgment of the universal level can be more readily given.

Since K. is constantly tormented by males, he turns to females for consolation. As the male figures of the trial form the group-father, so the females constitute the group-mother. Frau Grubach is the main mother surrogate. She is protective, possessive, and irrational in her dealings with her son. His arrest is nothing criminal to her; she dismisses it as something that she has no need to understand. Her only concern is for K.'s happiness. When the name of Fräulein Bürstner is mentioned, the mother is quick to recognize the possible breach in the mother-son relationship that another woman could cause, and she immediately places doubt in the son's mind concerning the moral standards of the girl. When K. becomes morose about Frau Grubach's statements, she does what she can to regain the graces of her son. That K., himself, thinks of Frau Grubach as a mother is emphasized by the detail: "K. sah, wie so oft, auf ihr Schürzenband nieder" (p. 26). Frau Grubach's avoidance of K.'s hand following their discussion of the arrest places doubts into his mind concerning his mother's acceptance of him.

It is at this point that he turns to Fräulein Bürstner. He felt no special desire to see her, he could not even remember exactly how she looked, but after being rejected by Frau Grubach, he wanted to talk to her. When he hears her return to the boarding house, he whispers her name through the door and "Es klang wie eine Bitte, nicht wie ein Anruf" (p. 35). This is K.'s prayer for acceptance by the female. In this sense, Fräulein Bürstner is the mother-image as the protector of the son from the father-tormentor. But K.'s attempt to gain favor from the mother again fails. Fräulein Bürstner rejects him as an immature child. That he is desperate for her acceptance is emphasized in his frantic attempt to make love to her; he "küsste sie auf den Mund und dann über das ganze Gesicht, wie ein durstiges Tier mit der Zunge über das endlich gefundene Quellwasser hinjagt" (p. 42). That their interlude is interrupted by Captain Lanz (the father as the normal sexual male) further inforces Fräulein Bürstner's role as a symbolic mother.

In K.'s vain attempt to make love to the wife of the Law-Court Attendant, the action of the Bürstner episode is repeated. Again the father-image, this time in the guise of the Examining-Magistrate, prohibits K. from being successful. In this scene, K. openly seeks to give vent to his lust for power over the father-image. Although the woman offers to aid K. in his trial, he actually puts no faith in her ability. It is the possiblility of wresting her from the father that makes her attractive. K. says that "... es gab vielleicht keine bessere Rache an dem Untersuchungsrichter und an seinem Anhang, als dass er ihnen diese Frau entzog und an sich nahm" (p. 72). However, K.'s attempt to gain the mother's love is again

70

frustrated when she is carried off to the Examining-Magistrate by the bandy-legged student.

With Leni, the Advocate's nurse, K. experiences his only sexual triumph. This apparent victory in his battle with the fathers is only an illusion. It is true that Leni willingly gives herself to K., but she does not love K. for himself. Her love is impersonal and inconsequential, for she finds all accused men equally attractive. K. has actually gained nothing. The father-advocate still exercises complete control over the mother-image.

In K.'s futile tossing about to find some way of shaking himself free from his arrest, these women play a special role. In each of them he sees the potentiality of freedom from the torment inflicted upon him by the father-figures, but in his dealings with them, this possibility is frustrated. Although they possess the independence and self-confidence that K. desires, his relationship with them as individuals is too casual to bring about positive results. Just as K. cannot perceive the difference between the worlds of authentic and unauthentic existence, he cannot see on the symbolic level of the battle with the fathers that the mother functions merely as an alleviator of pain or torture. She cannot lead him to complete understanding. The mother endeavors to aid her son in his progress toward self realization, but she places the total responsibility of that realization upon him. If in his ignorance he seeks to possess her not as a woman but as an object of revenge, she joins the father in the destruction of the son.

71

The same trinity of characters that clashes to bring about the action of *Der Prozess* also appears in *L'Etranger*. In Camus' work the father-mother-son relationship dominates the action of the book on the symbolic level. Meursault, as the son in defiance of socially accepted practice, goes swimming and begins a liaison with Marie the day following his mother's funeral. His father,[2] like K.'s, is deceased; but the dead father condemns his son's actions in the guise of the lawyer, the examining magistrate, the public prosecutor and the priest. In simple terminology the basic character and situation pattern of *L'Etranger* involves the young hero who murders, the mother-sweetheart who is directly involved in the hero's death and the father-figures who condemn him.[3]

To the father as an authoritarian (the lawyer, the examining magistrate and the public prosecutor), the fact that Meursault murdered an Arab is inconsequential. Meursault's crime, as he himself feels, is that he is "de trop." To these men, life is based upon a socially accepted formula. Man exists within a society that believes in the sanctity of motherhood and the grace of God. If he fails to adhere to these rules, he is not only outside the social pattern but is, in reality, a threat of destruction to that pattern. Meursault's crime is that he does not conform to the rules.[4] Again and again Meursault is questioned about the same things. The lawyer-father promises him his freedom if he follows his advice and lies about his reactions to his mother's death. He does not question Meursault about his crime but about the great callousness that he had shown at his mother's funeral. The only satisfaction that Meursault can give the lawyer is that he would prefer that his mother had not died. The lawyer, unable to get any expression of sympathy from Meursault, leaves him. Meursault's next contact is with the magistrate-father. The question that arises in this interview concerns Meursault's belief in God. Meursault denies any feeling for God and becomes bored with the conversation. The magistrate is no more capable of understanding Meursault than was the lawyer, and their discussion only affirms the magistrate's opinion that Meursault is a case-hardened criminal. In the figure of the public prosecutor the total effect of Meursault's actions upon society is made clear. Again, the fact that an Arab was killed is insignificant. Meursault's guilt is proved by placing his past life under the judgment of absolute moral standards. Here the father bombards the son with all the crimes that make him despicable to society. Meursault's heartlessness at his mother's funeral, his liaison with Marie, the Fernandel movie, the letter he had written in collusion with Raymond, his intelligence, his lack of a soul are all infinitely more significant than the real crime he committed. In his closing remarks to the jury, the prosecutor makes a statement that clarifies the symbolic level of the trial. Logically it is absurd. He asks that Meursault be convicted not only for the moral guilt of his mother's death but also for the guilt of the murder of his father. The authoritarian-father has condemned the son to death for his attempted reversal of the accepted order.

The father-son relationship between the priest and Meursault is even more obvious. The father openly accosts the son in the figure of the priest. Again the same questions are asked of Meursault, but it is during the final interview with the priest that Meursault is totally destroyed. Following his trial and conviction, Meursault still nurtured some hope for an appeal and eventual freedom. It is in his argument with the priest that Meursault's thoughts formulate. The father is not only unable to convince Meursault of the validity of Christian dogma, but he actually clarifies Meursault's disbelief. In his discussion with the priest, Meursault recognizes and acknowledges the finality of death. He knows that there is no escape from death and that the most wonderful thing that could happen would be to be able to begin life over again. It is true that the argument with the father results in Meursault's revolt and moment of clairvoyance, but at the same time this moment brings about the total destruction of the son. The father has succeeded in making the son aware of the impossibility of hope and the finality of death. The priest-father deals the death blow to Meursault.

Although the fathers actually condemn the son, it is the fatal attraction of the mother that brings about this condemnation. The entire court-jury reaction to Meursault is based upon his behavior at and following his mother's funeral. His treatment

74

of his mother is the real cause of his death. In other words, the mother is responsible for her son's condemnation. Marie, the only other important female character, is closely associated with the mother. The name itself is the name of Christ's mother. Subconsciously, at least, there must be a relationship in Camus' mind between Christ and the mother Mary and the Anti-Christ Meursault and his mother and Marie. Marie's function in the book also justifies an identification of her with Madame Meursault. She, too, is responsible for Meursault's guilt for it is she whom he meets at the beach, takes to the Fernandel movie, and sleeps with that night. It is also she who is with him the day of the murder.

In *L'Etranger*, as in *Der Prozess*, the father and the mother images join forces to bring about the son's death. The mother lures the son into the trap set by the father. By identifying the male and female characters of their novels with the mother and father, Kafka and Camus have symbolically presented the forces which often dominate the life of the ordinary individual. The social code in accordance with which man acts is first learned from his parents. If he cannot free himself from or re-evaluate this code, he remains forever fettered to unauthentic existence and dies like a dog. Contrariwise, if he revolts against parental authority, although still condemned, he becomes a sacrificial hero, an Anti-Christ, whose hope is that at his death other men will recognize the authenticity of his life and join in his revolt.

This duality of symbols which dominates the lives of K. and Meursault is also apparent in the natural symbols employed by both authors. The contest between authentic and unauthentic existence on the philosophical level and the mother-father-son relationship on the psychological level is repeated by the natural elements in which these other two levels function.

It is significant that the action of these novels takes place in the city. Only in the complexity of the modern city can the basic philosophic problem of these two works exist. It is in the turmoil of the city that man most poignantly feels his aloneness, his anxieties, and his despairs. K. and Meursault are surrounded by people, but communicate with none of them. They are apart. Although neither the city of *Der Prozess* nor Algiers is a prison, each functions as such. K. and Meursault are confined within the walls of man-made structures, and it is with these artificial aspects of civilization that they must deal. K. is free; yet the nature of his trial limits him to a world of tenement houses, tall buildings, and slums. Meursault, on the other hand, at first free to enjoy his natural surroundings, eventually discovers Algiers only through prison bars. As seen by K. and Meursault, this metropolitan décor becomes integrated into the narratives as a significant agent in the development of the novels. The landscape actually supports the action on the real and the symbolic levels. The darkness and airlessness of the city of *Der Prozess* and the sun and the sea of Algiers are as important

76

to the novels as any of the main characters; and, as might be expected, these natural phenomena also symbolically support the duality of the mother and father images.

The city of *Der Prozess* is a city void of light. For a year K. searches for truth in a world of mist and gloom in which guilt and innocence, irony and seriousness are impossible to distinguish one from the other. The only light is the artificial light of candles or the reflected light of the moon. The sun never shines. In a work that depends so heavily upon weather conditions to indicate the time-flow of the action, the absence of any mention of sunlight cannot be accidental. Perhaps the clearest explanation can be found in the meaning given to the sun in the religious myths of antiquity. The sun is the male principle, the symbol of God and of truth. There is no doubt that K.'s search is a search for truth. The various interpretations of the meaning of truth to Kafka may be questioned, but it is generally agreed that K. is in search of *a* truth that he never finds. The lack of sunlight in *Der Prozess* might very well symbolize the absence of truth for K. in the city of *Der Prozess*. This argument gains credibility if one recalls that the only bright light mentioned in the book emits from the door to truth in the legend of the doorkeeper.

The absence of sunlight symbolizes an absence of truth attainable to K.; and in keeping with this interpretation, it is striking to note that when K. most nearly approaches the realms of truth, the

world of authentic existence, the atmosphere of the
novel takes on those attributes generally related to
intense sunlight. In the interrogation chamber, in
the law-court offices, and in Titorelli's apartment,
the heat is so intense that it becomes unbearable
to K. In all three instances, K. is either in contact
with the court or near it. The court is, it will be
remembered, the clearest representation of the
world of real values. In the interrogation chamber,
K. feels the air too thick for him; in the law-court
offices, he comments on the dull and heavy
air and becomes nauseated by the heat; in
Titorelli's apartment he feels the air stifling
hot. In the first two instances, he is in
direct contact with the court offices; the third
would be somewhat inconsistent except that
Titorelli mentions that his studio really belongs to
the law-court offices. The sun never shines upon
K. in the city of *Der Prozess*; yet the intense heat
of the law-court offices is logically explained by
the hot sun beating on the roof. This explanation is
logical in the first instances, but K. visits Titorelli's apartment in winter when it is snowing
outside, and the oppressive air is inexplicable.
"... öfters hatte er schon verwundert auf einen
kleinen, zweifellos nicht geheizten Eisenofen in der
Ecke hingesehen, die Schwüle im Zimmer war
unerklärlich" (p. 178). The equating of sun and
light with truth, whether consciously done by the
author or not, is apparent.

As K. drifts farther away from the truth, there
is a total absence of the sun's attributes. In his

consultations with the lawyer Huld, the only light is supplied by candles, and it is so dark in Huld's chambers that K. cannot see sufficiently well to recognize that another person is present in the room. The same pitch darkness prevails in the cathedral scene. K. cannot see the paintings on the wall, he cannot see to find his way out, and the light that the priest gives him goes out in his hand. K.'s associations with the law and with the church are futile associations for him; he consequently remains literally and symbolically in the dark. That Huld and the priest are somehow related to the court does not alter the effectiveness of the symbol. K. learns nothing from his contact with them and remains far removed from the truth of the sun.

K.'s other contacts in the course of the trial are made with women, and it is significant that these contacts, with the exception of the law-court attendant's wife, are associated with the moon. The night that he sees Fräulein Bürstner, "Der Mond schien still in das dunkle Zimmer" (p. 32). With Leni the moonlight brilliantly lit up a small section of the floor. In the case of Fräulein Montag (the day of the moon), the meaning is obvious. The moon emits the reflected light of the sun, is a feminine symbol, and a cold, phlegmatic planet. The association of the moon with the feminine characters of the book reinforces their role in K.'s quest. They, too, are only reflections of truth; they can aid K., but they cannot actually give him understanding.

The use of the sun and moon as masculine and feminine symbols in Kafka's writing and the equating of the sun with truth can be illustrated. The duality of these natural symbols is in keeping with the duality of the realms of authentic and unauthentic existence and the duality of the mother and the father images. It is interesting to note further that the weakness of the female is present in the nature symbols as it is in the mother-father symbol. The moon shines in both the whipper scene and the final scene of the novel. Realistically, of course, the moonlight lends to the eerie and uncanny aspects of the scenes, but if it is true that K. casts about too much for help from females and that the female is only able to reflect the truth, the fact that she is present in the form of the moon in the two essentially masculine scenes and is mysteriously present behind a window on K.'s way to his death seems to reinforce her position of submissiveness to the masculine. K.'s final gesture to raise his hands and spread out all his fingers as if to make one last grasp at the heavens for some meaning to his life is futile, for he has failed to see the truth of the sun.

In contrast to the city of *Der Prozess*, Algiers is flooded by brilliant sunlight. That the sun is used by Camus as a symbol of ultimate vision or truth can best be explained by the relationship between the sun symbol and the three decisive acts of the book. The burial, the crime, and the trial all take place under the broiling rays of the sun. These are Meursault's three contacts with death, and it is

80

through an awareness of death that his destiny as
an individual is accomplished. Without death
there would be no problem for him to face; he
would simply be a part of the eternal natural order.
However, once aware of death and the finality of
his existence, his tragedy begins.[5]

In his initial contact with death, wherever
Meursault looked he saw the same sun-drenched
countryside, and the sky was so dazzling that he
dared not raise his eyes. His sensitive vision was
forced to concentrate upon the things of the earth:
the tarred road, the blackness of everything around
him and the smells of hot leather and of horse dung.
His reactions to the sun in this scene are passive.
In his usual way, he accepts the situation without
question. He takes delight in observing each detail,
but the only emotion he is capable of is his little
thrill of pleasure when he entered the streets of
Algiers and he pictured himself going to bed and
sleeping for twelve hours.

At the beach before he murdered the Arab, he
felt the same sort of heat as at his mother's funeral
and had the same disagreeable sensations, but he
was determined not to be beaten by the sun. The
sun pressed on him, trying to check his progress;
but each time he felt a hot blast strike his forehead,
he gritted his teeth, clenched his fists in his pockets
and keyed up every nerve to fend off the sun and
the dark befuddlement it was pouring into him.
There is no lack of emotion in the murder scene.
Under the scorching rays of the sun, Meursault
defies it and pits his strength against it. The heat

became so intense that his veins seemed to be bursting through his skin. It is at this moment that he stepped forward in a futile attempt to allay the sun. The Arab drew his knife and Meursault shot. It is the sun that drives Meursault to murder. Meursault's defiance of the sun is his expression of revolt against the forces that brought him to the act of murder.

In Meursault's last contact with death and the sun, at his trial, the air was stifling hot and the stuffiness of the air made him feel a bit dizzy. He was overcome by the heat and confused by what went on around him. He tried to explain that he murdered because of the sun, but he spoke too quickly, ran his words together and the people tittered. In the courtroom scene there is no real sun, no truth, just the attributes of truth as seen by men. Here the brilliant reds of the geraniums and tawny earth at the funeral and the glowing red of the sun at the time of the murder are replaced by the red gown of the presiding judge, the gaudy fans of the jurymen, the red penholder used to write the letter for Sintès, and the scarlet ears of the condemning Pérez. Just as the trial reflects the false values of a man-invented social order, the court scene materially reflects attributes of the sun. The court joins the sun in its condemnation of Meursault, but it is in no way a reflection of truth. The men of the court are never aware that the reality of death is a humiliating and incomprehensible phenomenon.

Meursault's three contacts with death are

illuminated by the sun. In the first instance, Meursault lowered his eyes from the blinding sun and ignored death. He went back to work as usual; really nothing in his life had changed. In his second contact with death, he was defiant of the sun. He wanted to eliminate death from his life, and the shots that he fired into the Arab were his futile attempt to alter the eternal order. After his trial, he resigned himself to his fate. He realized that all men must die and that death was the inexplicable bond between them. He learned that it could neither be ignored nor destroyed but had to be faced with defiance. The sun illuminates the central truth for Meursault and for all men, and in its role as condemner it joins the judge-prosecuting attorney-priest figure as a father image.

In contrast to the destructive powers of the sun, the sea offers solace to Meursault. In prison he speaks of his desire to go to the beach for a swim, and in his daydreams he imagines the sound of ripples at his feet, the smooth feel of water on his body, and the wonderful sensation of relief that water gives to him. As in ancient religious myths, water here, too, possesses purifying qualities that make man free of sin.

The sea is also identified with the mother image. Viggiani points out that *la mère* and *la mer* are homonyms and Marie "not only resembles the first two phonetically but is the name of the type of the mother, who has traditionally been associated with the sea.[6] To Meursault the sea also has the attributes of the mother. She gives solace to his tired body and he emerges from her as if born anew. However, as the mother, she, too, is a source of destruction. It is her fatal attraction that draws Meursault to the beach where he meets Marie and begins the liaison that is a key factor in his condemnation. It is also the sea that turns into molten steel the day of the murder and joins forces with the sun to possess Meursault and lead him into his undoing.

As in *Der Prozess*, in *L'Etranger* the nature symbols represent the dual aspects of existence. In the realm of unauthentic existence, Meursault is subjected to social dictates. His revolt against this authority is realistically portrayed in his accosting of the priest. The same action is symbolically presented in his firing of the gun against the sun. In both instances he revolts against the forces that dominate his life. In the first part of the book, Meursault's sensitivity to light is mentioned no less than fourteen times.[7] For a man to whom ideas have no significance, physical events alone are capable of influencing him and making him act. It is against these physical events that he revolts in his attempt to destroy the sun. In the second half of the book, Meursault begins to reflect; he is no longer a man without a past. Ideas become significant to him, and it is against the false ideas of society that he revolts when he openly accosts the priest. Expressed more factually, the father-figures ally with the sun symbol to bring about Meursault's death. As in *Der Prozess*, the mother

84

figures, here symbolically joined by the sea, aid in the condemnation.

Both *Der Prozess* and *L'Etranger* can be read as naturalistic pieces of writing, a fact which is a tribute to Kafka and Camus as story-tellers rather than a criticism of their ability to express a philosophical idea in fiction.[8] The books are first of all interesting tales that capture and hold the reader's attention from the beginning to the end. However, to interpret the books on a purely naturalistic level is invalid, and any temptation to do so soon disappears on close reading of the novels. Every detail within these carefully planned works points to a double meaning. K. and Meursault are not moronic automata who are manipulated from one point to another as pawns of a materialistic society. They are representations of valid human beings who endeavor to attain and defend a positive attitude toward life. K.'s world of darkness and airlessness is not only the eerie realm of nightmares and hallucinations; it is the city of the twentieth century which with all its exterior trappings hides the truth from the individual and forces him into an unauthentic existence. The inexplicable actions of the court-jury that tried Meursault underline the stupidity of social assumptions. In Meursault's inability to understand the court proceedings and in the reader's awareness of Meursault's actions before his trial, the judgment of society and the basis for that judgment are made ridiculous. In these books every level of society undergoes criticism. The mother and father assume the first responsibility for embedding false ideas into the minds of their children. On a symbolic level, K. and Meursault both contest these ideas. The fact that the family, the state, and the church eventually condemn the individual does not defeat his cause. It makes him into a sacrificial character whose death serves as an enlightenment to other men. Even names are used to communicate feelings. Erna, which means retiring, is a shy girl in *Der Prozess*. Masson in *L'Etranger* is "un grand type massif."[9] Colors, as we have seen, are also not chosen arbitrarily. Each detail and action in these books invites interpretation, and as Camus has said, there is no valid word for word correspondence between a symbol and its translation. With all the clues at one's disposal, still no absolute interpretation of the symbols can be made. The struggle depicted by Kafka and Camus of man against his fate is real, but the Protean aspects of the symbols make it easy for anyone to read his own problems and his own struggle into the life of K. or Meursault.

From the confrontation of K. and Meursault with
the worlds of *Der Prozess* and *L'Etranger*, one idea
emerges to dominate all others. Although each of
their actions ends in the defeat of the individual
and each defeat brings new frustrations to him,
both men are possessed by the urge to live. From
the instance of arrest in which he rejects the idea
of suicide, throughout the year of incomprehensible
entanglements with the court, until the final
moments of his life, K. struggles against resignation
to the cold indifference of the universe. It is only
after he is exhausted by his meaningless striving
and faced with inescapable death, that he calmly
and discriminatingly voices the thought that until
this time he had refused to recognize: "Die Logik
ist zwar unerschütterlich, aber einem Mensch, der
leben will, widersteht sie nicht" (p. 272)[1]. In the
last moment of his life, the one thing that really
matters to anyone is expressed in simple but
painful clarity by the condemned K. Regardless
of the price, man wants to go on living. This same
love of life is shared by the reticent Meursault in
L'Etranger. Beaten by an outdated social order
that compels an individual to conform by mouth
and not by deed, fully aware that there is no escape
from his pending execution, Meursault says, "... je
me suis senti prêt à tout revivre" (p. 171).

These are stange statements from men who
know that their destruction was partially caused by
the outdated dictates of society. K. and Meursault
are aware that society refused them the final rights
of judgment and denied them their importance as

individuals. They know that the absolute religious and social values by which they were judged are conventional and outworn. They are cognizant of all these things; yet, in full realization of the limitations of society, their final wish is not to withdraw from it but to resubject themselves to the tortuous entanglements of day-to-day living. The reason for this wish can only be explained by the one additional discovery made by K. and Meursault. Near death, they have learned that life with all its inexplicable involvements is not only worth living, but that it offers man his one chance for happiness. The absurdity of life, which actually has nothing to do with either society or man's behavior within society, cannot be denied or eradicated. It is in reality an invitation to a happiness completely rooted in the knowledge that men live and men die. K.'s and Meursault's thoughts echo those of Sisyphus, "La lutte elle-même vers les sommets suffit à remplir un cœur d'homme."[2]

The fight toward the summit for K. and Meursault demands almost superhuman endurance, for their discovery of the singular value of life does not occur until the last pages of the novels. They are dragged through defeat after defeat before they are able to acknowledge the one glaring truth that they chose to ignore throughout the major portions of the novels. *Der Prozess* and *L'Etranger* are novels of development in which the protagonists must go through the agonizing experience of affirming that the infinite value of life lies in the very finiteness of its nature. K. and Meursault, although they conduct their lives according to polar value standards, essentially experience the same stages of development. For both of them, the existence which they had been leading is brought into question; they both reject the rational explanation of man's position proffered by the law and the irrational appeal of religious dogma; in spite of constant personal defeat by the complexities of day-to-day living, both reject suicide and affirm the value of life; finally, as a consequence of their failure to surmount or eradicate the finiteness of existence, they recognize the absurdity of life and the potentiality of man gains new dignity through this recognition.

From the moment of K.'s and Meursault's arrest, the world in terms of their experience becomes inexplicable to them. According to the accepted standards of society by which K. had meticulously conducted his life, there is no basis for his arrest. Meursault finds himself in a comparable position. He had based his actions upon complete indifference to everything except physical sensations; and projecting this philosophy to the extreme, he saw no difference between firing and not firing the shots into the body of the Arab. Both K. and Meursault are abruptly introduced to a world that is inexplicable in the terms of their understanding. The moment of the clash of the opposed demands of their individual moral codes and the social codes by which they are judged initiates the gradual awakening of K. and Meursault to the absurdity of the universe.

Before either K. or Meursault acknowledges the unauthenticity of his own existence, he endeavors to strike out against the society which has placed him in confinement. K., in accordance with the only frame of reference he knows, attempts to find a rational explanation for his arrest in the law, the arts, and the church; but each contact results in failure. Meursault, in agreement with his way of life, does not actively seek an explanation for his arrest; however, by being placed in confinement, he is automatically exposed to the same set of values that K. searches out. In neither case does the law or the church resolve the conflict; but since they are the agents responsible for the condemnation of K. and Meursault, they are the instruments which lead the men to a positive affirmation of the value of life.[3] In their quest for some meaning to life, it is at the moment of imminent death that K. and Meursault finally turn from exterior forces inward to themselves. K. attempted to conduct his life in agreement with an out-worn social code. He questioned everything without taking the individual into account. Until the final moments of his life, he hoped that he could transcend the limitations of human existence through exterior agencies. Finally aware of the inability of a social code to solve the conflict between his desire to go on living and his inescapable death, K., in a flash of clairvoyance that has the potency of a religious revelation,

90

expresses his first unconditioned response when he says that logic cannot withstand a man who wants to go on living. Meursault, too, although he chose to transform rather than conform to the world, dies knowing that he has failed. Throughout his life, he refused to question anything. Hoping to transform the world by ignoring its limitations, he accepted only the sensual aspects of life. At the time of his death he realizes for the first time that happiness cannot exist in a world where all actions are equal. He discovers in death that in the face of the absurd fact that all men must die, no one man can afford just to exist. To fail to question the meaning of life is to condemn the individual and the world to nothingness.

K. and Meursault are, above all else, men who want to go on living. From the opening scene of *Der Prozess* in which K. rejects the opportunity to take his own life until the final scene in which he perceives that he is to commit suicide, the idea that he expresses early in the book, "Es wäre so sinnlos gewesen, sich umzubringen, dass er selbst wenn er es hätte tun wollen, infolge der Sinnlosigkeit dazu nicht imstande gewesen wäre" (p. 17) dominates all of his actions. K. cannot let go of life, for to let go would mean that he understood it in all its complexities. K. understands only one thing. Through all his painful experiences, the only positive fact that he can cling to is an intuitive feeling that life is good and that the absence of all hope in a future existence intensifies its value. In *L'Etranger* Meursault shares K.'s love of life. No matter how unbearable prison life becomes for him, death is never a temptation. Life at any price is worth the living. Meursault's desire for life is most clearly expressed when he says, "J'ai souvent pensé alors que si l'on m'avait fait vivre dans un tronc d'arbre sec, sans autre occupation que de regarder la fleur du ciel au-dessus de ma tête, je me serais peu à peu habitué (p. 110).

These men are everyday men – an officer of a bank and an office clerk – who are suddenly interrupted in the hopes and ambitions of an ordinary life and brought to a painful realization that death is an inescapable fact. In their day-to-day living, their personal relationship with the world had never been brought into question. K., in his obsession with bussiness success and Meursault in his thorough enjoyment of each sensual pleasure had never thought of the time when these experiences would be ended by death. It is at the moment of arrest that both of them are jarred out of their feeling of complacency and are forced to think of themselves in association with the world. That they cannot immediately accept the nature of the relationship between man and the universe is explicable in the terms of the false social order to which they were subjected. The feeling of absurdity that arises from the clash of the desire of the human mind that the world should be explicable in human terms and the fact that the world is not thus understandable becomes present in the thoughts of K. and Meursault throughout *Der Prozess* and *L'Etranger*. But the absurdity of

92

the universe is not unconditionally accepted by
them until the last pages of the novels. They, as
representatives of every man, must seek out, be
subjected to, and finally reject all the time-
honored answers offered to solve man's enigmatic
relationship to his universe. In their search for a
meaning to life, the one positive conclusion that
both K. and Meursault finally come to is that life
is finite. Nowhere within this world can they find
any proof of a life beyond the grave. K. and Meursault know that they exist and that the world
exists, and they become increasingly aware that
anything beyond these two tangible facts is mere
construction. They toss about from the purely
sensual to the logical to the religious, but nowhere
are they able to find anything but paradox.
Every new adventure reinforces the illogic of the
earth. K. and Meursault discover but one truth
concerning human existence: "Une vérité toute
simple et toute claire, un peu bête, mais difficile
à découvrir et lourde à porter ... Les hommes
meurent et ils ne sont pas heureux."[4] K.'s and
Meursault's search for truth, unity, and a meaning
to life is constantly blocked by the irrational
world. Finally faced with imminent death, exhausted by a fruitless battle waged in an attempt
to alter the unalterable, they are forced to accept
the doctrine of absurdity. They relinquish all
efforts to transcend or destroy the limitations of
human existence and submit to an indifferent
nature that remains forever distinct from and
foreign to the nature of man.

93

In *Der Prozess* and *L'Etranger* the acceptance of
the doctrine of the absurd in no way implies
disdain of the universe.[5] Throughout the novels
K. and Meursault cling to the strange, fascinating
beauty of a world that they cannot comprehend.
The warmth of a female body, the odors of the sea,
the haunting light of the moon are, in fact, those
things which make life worth living for K. and
Meursault. Rather than a rejection of the universe,
K.'s and Meursault's rage to live is deeply rooted in
a total acceptance of the natural universe. What
they learn through their contacts with the superimposed structures of false society is that man is
alone and that all his actions are equally un-
important and insignificant in their effect upon
the nature of the universe. All men must die, and
K. and Meursault realize that nothing can be done
to alter the course of human existence. They
finally cease searching for some possible escape
from their human fate and totally resign themselves to the grandeur of the universe. They
cannot understand the relationship between man
and the world, but somehow – repeating the
intuitive feelings of Frau Grubach and Marie –
they no longer need to understand it.[6]

In addition they realize through their contacts
with unauthentic existence that all men are
oppressed by external values which have nothing
to do with either the nature of man or the nature of
the universe. Man's life is ruled by outdated
pretentions which should, as the men who created
them, be disintegrated into ashes. K.'s and

Meursault's recognition of the fact that the op-
pression of man is something he can act upon is
the beginning of their revolt.[7] For K. and Meursault this feeling of revolt comes too late to have
any positive results in their lives. K. has learned
that logic cannot provide all the answers to the
human condition; and Meursault, proceeding a
step further, has clearly formulated his feelings
of revolt. By implication, in K.'s hope that the
shame of his death will somehow outlive him and
in Meursault's wish that he be greeted by howls of
execration at his execution, an invitation is
offered to mankind for a life freed from involvement in the outworn dictates of twentieth-century
civilization. Through K.'s and Meursault's failure
as individuals, they offer positive hope to the rest
of mankind. Their entire existence was squandered
in a quest for a meaning to life that they finally
discovered near the time of their death. However,
this waste of human effort was not the fault of
either K. or Meursault but of an out-worn social
code which made no provisions for the deviations
in man's actions. The invitation offered by K. and
Meursault to all men is that they cease their
attempt to conquer the unconquerable, that they
acknowledge the absurdity of life, and that in full
recognition of the limitations placed upon mankind
they seek to build a new society that once again
acknowledges the dignity of man above all else.[8]

The implication underlying the theme of *Der
Prozess* and *L'Etranger* is that a world in which God
is dead and destiny is a human affair need not be

an unhappy world. From the individual recognition of the absurdity of life emerges a happiness which is neither sensual nor transcendent but which is the affirmation of the dignity and unique value of human life. In a world which offers no hope to mankind, man learns through the double consciousness of his desire for duration and his destiny of death to count on nothing and to consider the present as the only truth given to him.[9] From the consciousness that he is his own end and the only end to which he can aspire, it is right for man to question, but this questioning must result in an affirmation of the world of true values. Kafka's and Camus' basic attack is directed against the unnecessary suffering entailed by man in his relationships with his fellow man. They plead for recognition of the tragic journey of life and for the recognition on the part of man that he is not an isolated being. They are appalled by the blindness of man not only because he refuses to recognize the tragedy of human life but also because he refuses to see the value of acting decently upon it. Man's questioning alone leads him to frustration and resultant pessimism, but this pessimism must be a point of departure which takes him out of his individual despair to the recognition that the transitoriness of life is the link of solidarity he has with all mankind. Once he is aware that he does not have to battle alone, he can combine his force with that of all other men to re-establish human dignity.

All the actions of K. and Meursault in *Der*

96

Prozess and *L'Etranger* highlight the major tragedy of the twentieth century. In man's failure to question himself, he denies the one thing that could restore his human dignity. Frustrated and bored by the external aspects of the world that crushes him, without once realizing that he is a member of the only species that can express its frustration and boredom in words, he must not conform to or ignore these aspects. The sacrifice of K. and Meursault to a society which attempted to repress their individualities is Kafka's and Camus' plea to mankind that it recognize and alleviate the tragedy of the twentieth century. The man who fails to question himself is dead while he yet lives. The hope that Kafka and Camus offer is that the individual invest his energies in the betterment of the one positive fact to which he can cling: his life on this earth, in this moment.

[1] Camus, Personal Letter, Paris, le 3 déc. 1951. "J'ai lu Kafka à 25 ans et LE PROCÈS m'a frappé."

[2] Roger Quillot, *La Mer et les prisons: Essai sur Albert Camus* (Paris: Gallimard, 1956), p. 8.

[3] Germaine Brée, *Camus* (New Brunswick: Rutgers University Press, 1959), p. 195. "The essay on Kafka was not included in the first edition of *Le Mythe de Sisyphe*. Published separately in 1943 (L'Arbalète, Lyons), it was included in a later edition of *Sisyphe* to which it orginally belonged."

[4] *La Peste* (Paris: Gallimard, 1947), p. 51. "... je lisais ce roman. Voilà un malheureux qu'on arrête un matin, tout d'un coup. On s'occupait de lui et il n'en savait rien. On parlait de lui dans des bureaux, on inscrivait son nom sur des fiches. Vous trouvez que c'est juste. Vous trouvez qu'on a le droit de faire ça à un homme?

"Cela dépend, dit Rieux. Dans un sens, on n'a jamais le droit, en effet. Mais tout cela est secondaire. Il ne faut pas rester trop longtemps enfermé. Il faut que vous sortiez."

[5] Wilhelm Emrich, *Franz Kafka* (Bonn: Athenäum-Verlag, 1958), p. 420.

[6] Jean-Paul Sartre, "Explication de l'Etranger," *Cahiers du Sud* (Février, 1943), pp. 14-17.

[7] Thomas Hanna, *The Thought and Art of Albert Camus* (Chicago: Henry Regnery Co., 1958), pp. 145-148. Mr. Hanna evolves an interesting comparison of the opinions of Pierre Neraud de Boisdeffre, Germaine Brée, Michel Mohrt, and Rachel Bespaloff concerning the philosophical character of Camus' plays and novels.

[8] Sartre, *op. cit.*, p. 20.

[9] Philip Thody, *Albert Camus: A Study of His Work* (London: Hamish Hamilton, 1957), p. 112.

[10] Carl A. Viggiani, "Camus' L'Etranger," *Publications of the Modern Language Association*, LXXI (December, 1956), p. 885.

[11] Heinz Politzer, *Franz Kafka, Parable and Paradox* (Ithaca: Cornell University Press, 1962), pp. 334-356.

[12] Camus, "L'Espoir et l'absurde dans l'œuvre de Franz Kafka," *Le Mythe de Sisyphe* (Paris: Gallimard, 1942), p. 189.

[13] Kafka, *Beschreibung eines Kampfes* (N.Y.: Schocken Books, 1947), p. 121.

[14] Camus, *Le Mythe de Sisyphe* (Paris: Gallimard, 1942), p. 32.

[1] *L'Etranger* (Paris: Gallimard, 1942), p. 9.

[2] Brée, *op. cit.*, p. 105. "The tempo of the narrative in *L'Etranger* is an essential feature in its composition. The short, unconnected factual sentences in the opening pages reflect Meursault's relation to time: each successive sensation is registered with each successive moment; time, when Meursault is aware of it, is thus a discontinuous succession of moments, and for days at a stretch it drops out of his consciousness altogether."

[3] Viggiani, *op. cit.*, p. 868.

[4] The characters are not seen in any perspective other than the one given to them by K. and Meursault. For example, Block in *Der Prozess* is only met in the unfavorable atmosphere of the lawyer's home and is seen as a weak, insignificant pawn of the court officials. Marie in *L'Etranger* embodies the tender warmth of a loving female; however there is no other aspect of her personality developed.

[5] There is much in these novels that tends to be an abolishment of the conventional horizon in favor of the depiction of a more fundamental existence. This point alone undoubtedly accounts for the temptation of many readers to interpret these works as unreal. In much the same way as the painters of the generation of the *valori plastici* in Italy sought to discover the existence of an objective world which calls for a new twist, Kafka and Camus also tend toward a recreation of the objective world. They search for and attain a depiction of fundamental existence more exact perhaps than the world depicted by the exhausting realists. The definite architectural composition in paintings such as those by Giorgio de Chirico may be compared to the clear, concise structure used by Kafka and Camus in their novels. There is vivid language to be compared to bold color; definite statements to architectural composition; the unfathomable to the enigma.

[6] Albert Maquet, *Albert Camus ou l'invincible été* (Paris: Gallimard, 1956), pp. 43-44. "Chaque phrase, comme

chaque instant, forme un tout, un petit univers homogène et clos que rien ne rattache à ce qui précède et qui n'entraine rien dans son sillage. Sitôt énoncée, sitôt engloutie dans le silence. De l'une à l'autre, aucune articulation logique, aucune relation; dans leur juxtaposition, aucune trace d'une quelconque emprise de l'esprit sur le réel. A travers ce pointille verbal, les choses, les êtres, les faits nous atteignent isolément, nus, défilés, dépourvus de signification."

[7] In further agreement with Albert Maquet, it must be pointed out that: "Toujours est-il qu'à certains moments, dans certaines pages, le style attendri et chaleureux du poète de *Noces* réapparait furtivement, comme si le flux saccade et terne de l'esthétique absurde s'ouvrait parfois pour laisser affleurer, lumineux et ample, le débit de ses profondeurs." *Ibid.*, p. 45.

[8] Viggiani, *op. cit.*, p. 870. "The Oedipus myth is reflected in the complicated trap set for Meursault by chance, the sea, and the sun, and in his final attitude of reconciliation."

[9] Brée, *op. cit.*, p. 107. "The apparent realism of Camus' novels is thus somewhat misleading, for by every means at his disposal Camus creates closed worlds which recall the closed, self-contained universe of classical tragedy. Each of these worlds poses a problem, asks a question, which the main characters embody."

[10] In *L'Etranger* the murder is not a commonplace as such; however, the tone of the book suggests that the men trying Meursault found the act neither monstrous nor unusual. "Ce n'est pas l'homme qui a tué un autre homme 'à cause du soleil' que la société condamne, mais bien cette espèce de monstre qui se refuse avec une fermeté sans égale à entrer dans le jeu de ses illusions, de ses mensonges, de ses hypocrisies. On attend de lui une attitude rassurante, et il ne fait que dénoncer, par son obstination tranquille à dire la vérité, le visage réel, misérable de la condition humaine." Maquet, *op. cit.*, p. 41.

11 See H. Uyttersprot, *Eine Neue Ordnung der Werke Kafkas?* (Antwerpen : C. De Vries-Brouwers, 1957).

12 The use of every-day language, counterpoint and irony, although not narrative devices, are essential and comparable stylistic techniques in *Der Prozess* and *L'Etranger.*

[1] René Dauvin, *"The Trial:* Its Meaning," *Franz Kafka Today,* ed. Angel Flores and Homer Swander (Madison: The University of Wisconsin Press, 1958), p. 152.

[2] Frau Grubach's interpretation of the arrest is misunderstood by K. in the same way that the warders' removing of K.'s linens and eating his bread and honey are misinterpreted by him. Both of these incidents are meant as invitations to K. to leave his rational, material world, but K. is incapable of seeing them as such. There is no communication possible between K. and authentic existence. The fact that neither Frau Grubach nor the inspector shakes K.'s hand symbolically emphasizes this lack of communication.

[3] Charles Neider, *The Frozen Sea* (New York: Oxford University Press, 1948), p. 163. "The magistrate's books prove to be indecent – at least that is what K. thinks. But he is still unaware that he is dealing with a libidinous court. The indecent picture in the first book is childishly drawn. The title of the second is meaningful: *How Grete was Plagued by Her Husband Hans.* Grete (from Margaret) means pearl or child of the light. Hans (from Johannes) means the Lord graciously giveth or Jehovah is gracious. The noble names suggest the nobility of the libido. The intention of the book is thus not obscene. But K., to whom the genital is repugnant, regards it as such."

[4] Dauvin, *op. cit.*, p. 154.

[5] Herbert Tauber, *Franz Kafka* (New Haven: Yale University Press, 1948), p. 115. "The first way out is dependent on the attempts at defining comprehensively the relationships of existence that break down time and again owing to the limited reference of human speech. The second is dependent on the possibility of a human curtailment of a wide-open connection with the unknown. Both these ways out obviate the real acquittal, in that they represent only the human definition of the relationship."

6 Max Brod's identification of *Der Prozess* and *Das Schloss* as two manifested forms of the Godhead – justice and grace – removes the field of striving from the human into the spiritual realm. This interpretation is based more upon the events of Kafka's personal life than upon those of the novels, for these works are clear presentations of the real trial man undergoes to understand life within its own limits.

7 K.'s inability to understand the significance of the legend is emphasized symbolically. The lamp the priest gives him to carry goes out in his hand.

8 Tauber, *op. cit.*, p. 90. "A fundamental disappointment is not encountered until the experience of death, which detaches the man, removes him out of all the vain-speaking of the world, and delivers him up, forlorn and without hope in his menaced state, to his unfulfilled urge towards significance. Then man sees himself, not in the inexhaustible march of time, but in the decisive importance of the present moment."

9 The contradiction that arises here between this statement and those that precede and follow is obvious. However, as is so often true when speaking of Kafka, the paradox cannot be avoided. K. is at one and the same time an animal void of the dignity of man and a sacrificial character with the nobility of an Oedipus. From within the confines of the book, K., as a product of mass pressures, projects beyond his own limitations only at the brief moment before his death. At this time, he realizes the full value of human life, and almost simultaneously he is sacrificed to the meaningless dictates of twentieth-century society. In complete understanding of K.'s failure to go beyond his social conditioning, the reader sees him as a victim of a fate every bit as overpowering as that which controlled the destiny of Oedipus.

10 K.'s anguish is a direct reflection of Kafka's personal life. Kafka was a strange personality who from childhood struggled with the difficulty of being. He

104

was a delicate boy surrounded by three tyrannical females and a father who sought an heir in his weakling son. Kafka never attained the synthesis of his father's dynamic bourgeois existence and his mother's ascetic world of dreams. He was furthermore always aware of his physical unattractiveness; he felt himself apart from the gay world of his fellow students at the German elementary school in the Fleischmarkt and the German grammar school in the Old Town Square. As is clear from reading his diaries, everyday incidents took on momentous proportions for him. Year by year his fear of the outside world made him withdraw more within himself. His individuality increased and caused him insurmountable difficulties. He was forced to struggle against a family and a society which sought to eradicate his particularity. He rebelled against his father and he rebelled against organized religion, but the result of his rebellion was a feeling of guilt. He sought to be independent but was too weak to make a complete denial. He both denied and affirmed without daring to make a choice. He lived in anguish. Although his ideas conflicted with those of his father, he never ceased to desire parental approval. Kafka condemned Judaism, but he was never able to free himself from it. He damned and desired society at the same moment. It had no category to fit the independent, but only through it could he gain approval. No matter what Kafka chose, he felt himself wrong and punished himself for his choice.

[11] Camus, Personal Letter, Paris, le 3 déc. 1951. "J'ai lu Kafka à 25 ans. ... LE PROCÈS m'a frappé, l'œuvre complète m'a donné l'idée d'un écrivain extrêmement limité. Pour vous donner un exemple clair, je considère que Melville s'est proposé la même entreprise que Kafka mais y a réussi parce qu'il l'a inscrite à la fois dans l'ombre et le soleil; Kafka ne sort pas de la nuit."

[12] Charles Blanchard, "Camus, Albert," *Dictionnaire des contemporains*, p. 39. "L'existence est mensongère ou

elle est éternelle. A partir du moment ou l'on opte pour la première proposition : l'existence est mensongère (mais elle est, c'est l'essence qu'il nie, faisant ainsi profession d'existentialisme) il n'y a que deux solutions : la refuser ... ou l'accepter, et accepter par là toutes les conséquences d'un univers absurde en contradiction permanente avec l'appétit logique de l'homme. Ce conflict implique la résignation ou la révolte. Camus, et c'est ce qui le différencie de Kafka (du moins de l'attitude explicite de ses personnages), choisit la révolte. 'Je tire de l'absurde trois conséquences : ma révolte, ma liberté et ma passion.'"

This significant contrast between K. and Meursault is somewhat explained by the contrasting personal lives of Kafka and Camus. Kafka always felt himself apart from an active engagement in life; however, as is clear from his preface to a new and limited edition of his first book, *L'Envers et l'endroit*, Camus was always enchanted by the beauty and splendor of life: "... poverty was never a misfortune for me: it was always counterbalanced by the richness of light. And, because it was free from bitterness, I found mainly reasons for love and compassion in it. Even my rebellions at the time were illuminated by this light. They were essentially – and I think I can say it without misrepresentation – rebellions in favor of others. It is not certain that my heart was naturally inclined to this kind of love. But circumstances helped me and, to correct my natural indifference, I was placed halfway between poverty and the sun. Poverty prevented me from judging that all was well in the world and in history, the sun taught me that history was not all. I wanted to transform life, yes, but not the world, which was my god. And that is no doubt how I began this uncomfortable career in which I find myself, starting out with innocence on a fine line of equilibrium along which today I advance with difficulty without being sure I shall reach my goal. In other

words, I became an artist... Later, even when a
serious illness temporarily took this vital force away
from me, in spite of invisible infirmities and the weak-
nesses they brought me, I may have known fear or
discouragement but never bitterness. This illness
doubtless added other very serious impediments to
those I already had. But in the long run it fostered a
freedom of heart, the slight distance with regard to
human interests which saved me from resentment. This
privilege, since I have been living in Paris, I know to be
royal. But it is a fact that I have savored it to the full
and that, at least up to the present, it has illuminated
my life." Quoted in Brée, *op. cit.*, pp. 60-62.

13 Albert Camus, "Avant Propos" to *L'Etranger* (New
York: Appleton Century Crofts, 1955), p. viii. "Meursault, for me, is a poor and naked man, in love with the
sun which leaves no shadows. He is far from being
totally deprived of sensitivity for he is animated by a
passion, profound because it is tacit, the passion for the
absolute and for truth. It is still a negative truth, the
truth of being and feeling, but a truth without which
no conquest of the self or of the world is possible."

14 Jean-Paul Sartre, *op. cit.*, p. 10. Sartre's explication
of *L'Etranger* claims that *Le Mythe de Sisyphe* is
necessary to the understanding of *L'Etranger*: however,
the book is explicable without reference to *Le Mythe*.
The terminology used in *Le Mythe* is often wrongly
applied to the interpretation of *L'Etranger*. Meursault
actually does not become "l'homme absurde" until the
final page of the book.

15 *Le Mythe de Sisyphe*, p. 88.

16 Brée, *op. cit.*, p. 111. "Meursault is the man who
answers but never asks a question, and all his answers
alarm a society which cannot bear to look at the truth."

17 In the beginning of the book, Meursault seems to have
achieved the state of total passivity; yet he was once
a student in Paris and presumably had not always lived
in this way.

[18] Quillot, *op. cit.*, p. 98. "Alors vient la paix – non pas la paix divine – mais la paix du monde, tendre dans son indifférence et fraternel dans sa pérennité. Une certaine continuité du désespoir a engendré un bonheur qu'avait connu OEdipe."

[19] Brée, *op. cit.*, p. 113.

[20] Tauber, *op. cit.*, p. 119. "The real level of significance of this death is not to be found in a general, objective reality, in which the event could be definable, possibly as a magical intervention of the beyond, but in K.'s inner consciousness of his nullity. That is why it is said that K. should really kill himself. But that he cannot bring himself to do. The nullity of man without a foundation is only one of the contradictory perspectives of existence. In contrast with it appears the foundationless affirmation of an own vital immediacy as the true mode of existence corresponding to the character of the world. Suicide would be a transcending of these oppositions, but thereby immediately an act of faith, a true contact with the Court."

[21] Huld remarks to K. while discussing K.'s trial, "... es ist oft besser, in Ketten, als frei zu sein," p. 227.

[1] *Le Mythe de Sisyphe*, p. 173. "Un symbole est toujours dans le général et, si precise que soit sa traduction, un artiste ne peut y restituer que le mouvement: il n'y a pas de mot à mot."

[2] Meursault's single remark about his father concerns his father's reaction to an execution. To illustrate the importance of the theme of capital punishment to Camus, one need only refer to his 1957 essay, "Réflexions sur la Guillotine." "Abhorrence for capital punishment is one of the main – one might almost say *the* main – theme of Camus's work. It occurs in his first essays, in The Outsider and in The Myth of Sisyphus ('the opposite of a man who commits suicide is a man condemned to death'), is central to the message of The Plague, and dominates the whole of Camus's political thinking." Thody, *op. cit.*, p. 121.

[3] Viggiani, *op. cit.*, pp. 874-876, sees the same relationship in all of Camus' writings.

[4] Hanna, *op. cit.*, p. 42. "It is not an absurd universe which destroys Meursault; it is a moral legalism which has injected fixed values into a sphere which has no fixed moral values, i.e., human life."

[5] Viggiani, *op. cit.*, p. 883. "In social terms for Camus, murder, or death, is the door through which man enters history. Without death there would be no human history: 'L'injustice, la fugacité, la mort se manifestent dans l'histoire. En les repoussant, on repousse l'histoire elle-même' (*L'Homme révolté*, p. 357)".

[6] "The figure of the mother appears in some form in all of Camus' creative works, even if only in a passing reference, as in *Noces*. In *Le Malentendu* she murders the son by drowning him; in *L'Etranger* she is ultimately responsible for the son's death; she replaces the dying wife in *La Peste*; she is the long-suffering mother of Victoria in *L'Etat de Siège*; in *Les Justes* she appears as the wife of the Grand Duke, whom Ivan has blown up. Only for *Caligula* is it necessary to invoke the benevolent shade of Freud to find the mother, this time in

the figure of Drusilla, Caligula's sister, with whom he has had incestuous relations, and whose death sends him into a homicidal frenzy. The figure of the young sweetheart-wife-sister is also omnipresent, and plays as important a role in the recurring death ritual as the mother, either suffering death or its consequences, as in *La Peste* and *Le Malentendu*, or deliberately or otherwise bringing the hero closer to death, as in *L'Etranger* where the bathing and movie episodes help seal Meursault's fate, and in *Les Justes*, in which Dora makes the bomb that Kaliayev throws. The sister appears in one of Camus' works, *Le Malentendu*, and is mentioned as the cause of the hero's madness in *Caligula*. In both plays she is intimately associated with the mother, consciously in the first play, where she shares with her the role of murderess, and unconsciously in *Caligula*, in which she is the object of incestuous desires." *Ibid.*, p. 875.

[7] Hanna, *op. cit.*, p. 43.

[8] Thody, *op. cit.*, p. 171. "It is interesting to note that when *The Outsider* was first published, a few months before the *Myth of Sisyphus*, two of the critics who reviewed it saw it as a naturalistic piece of writing."

[9] Neider, *op. cit.*, and Viggiani, *op. cit.*, have done an interesting analysis of the meaning of names in Kafka's and Camus' works.

¹ Thody, *op. cit.*, p. 5, cites the following quotation from Camus: "Pour un esprit absurde, la raison est vaine et il n'y a rien au-delà de la raison."

² *Le Mythe de Sisyphe.* p. 168.

³ The reader, obliged by the artistic technique of Kafka and Camus, is led into immediate sympathy with the protagonists. Through the functioning of the courts and the church in both trials, the reader becomes increasingly aware of the mechanical and preconceived structure of society. The rigid pattern by which man must live and the false hopes proffered by religion for man's salvation are made to seem ridiculous in their inability to aid K. and Meursault.

⁴ *Caligula* (Paris: Gallimard, 1944), p. 111.

⁵ Hanna, *op. cit.*, p. 48. "... what is most obvious is that Meursault is not revolting against the absurdity of the world; rather, he is revolting against the attitude which holds that human life is to be governed and judged according to autonomous principles which are lasting and sovereign."

⁶ The women of the novels play a role that contrasts to that of the protagonists. They find their composure in love or in a need for belonging. Intellectually they question very little, but they have an intuitive feeling that man independent of other men can solve nothing. They have been able to attain a composure for which the men strive.

⁷ Thody, *op. cit.*, p. 26. "The important difference between the attitude of the absurd and that of revolt lies in their fertility and in the realms of their application. The absurd is essentially an individual sensation. It is experienced by the individual conscience and its rules are applicable only to individual cases. Revolt, on the other hand, although at the very beginning an individualistic movement, can only really come to life by passing beyond the individual, and will inevitably be concerned with politics and political action."

111

[8] *Le Mythe de Sisyphe*, pp. 120-121. "Oui, l'homme est sa propre fin. Et il est sa seule fin. S'il veut être quelque chose, c'est dans cette vie. … Visages tendus, fraternité menacée, amitié si forte et si pudique des hommes entre eux, ce sont les vraies richesses puisqu'elles sont périssables. C'est au milieu d'elles que l'esprit sent le mieux ses pouvoirs et ses limites."

[9] Hanna, *op. cit.*, p. 8.

BIBLIOGRAPHY

Works by Franz Kafka

Amerika. New York: Schocken Books, Inc., 1947.
Beschreibung eines Kampfes. New York: Schocken Books, Inc., 1947.
Briefe Kafkas, 1900-1924. New York: Schocken Books, Inc., 1958.
Briefe an Milena. New York: Schocken Books, Inc., 1952.
Erzählungen und kleine Prosa. New York: Schocken Books, Inc., 1947.
Hochzeitsvorbereitungen auf dem Lande und andere Prosa aus dem Nachlass. New York: Schocken Books, Inc., 1953.
Der Prozess. New York: Schocken Books, Inc., 1947.
Das Schloss. New York: Schocken Books, Inc., 1947.
Tagebücher, 1910-1923. New York: Schocken Books, Inc., 1949.

Criticism of Kafka's Work

Ackermann, Paul Kurt. "A History of Critical Works on Franz Kafka," *German Quarterly* (March, 1950), pp. 104-113.
Anders, Günther. *Kafka, Pro und Contra*. Munich: C. H. Beck, 1951.
Auden, W. H. "Kafka's Quest," *The Kafka Problem*, ed. A. Flores. New York: New Directions, 1946. Pp. 47-52.
Bergel, Lienhard. "The Burrow," *The Kafka Problem*, ed. A. Flores. New York: New Directions, 1946. Pp. 199-206.
— "*Amerika:* Its Meaning," *Franz Kafka Today*, ed. A. Flores. Madison: The University of Wisconsin Press, 1958. Pp. 117-126.
Bithell, Jethro. *Modern German Literature*. London: Methuen, 1939. Pp. 406-411.

113

Blanchot, Maurice. "Kafka et l'exigence de l'œuvre," *L'Espace Littéraire*. Paris: Gallimard, 1955. Pp. 52-81.

Brod, Max. *Franz Kafka, eine Biographie*. Prague: Heinrich Mercy Sohn, 1935.

— "Epilogue," *The Trial*. New York: Knopf, 1937. Pp. 291-297.

— "Afterword," *Amerika*. New York: New Directions, 1940. Pp. 298-299.

— "The Homeless Stranger," *The Kafka Problem*, ed. A. Flores. New York: New Directions, 1946. Pp. 179-180.

— "Bemerkungen zu Kafkas *Schloss*," *Neue Züricher Zeitung* (October 20, 1951), p. 5.

Burgum, Edwin Berry. "Kafka and the Bankruptcy of Faith," *Accent* (Spring, 1943), pp. 153-167.

Camus, Albert. "L'Espoir et l'absurde dans l'œuvre de Franz Kafka," *Le Mythe de Sisyphe*. Paris: Gallimard, 1942. Pp. 173-189.

Carrouges, Michel. *Franz Kafka*. Paris: Librairie Editions Labergerie, 1948.

Daniel-Rops. "A French Catholic Looks at Kafka," *Thought* (September, 1948), pp. 401-404.

— "The Castle of Despair," *The Kafka Problem*, ed. A. Flores. New York: New Directions, 1946. Pp. 184-191.

Dauvin, René. "The Trial: Its Meaning," *Franz Kafka Today*, ed. A. Flores. Madison: The University of Wisconsin Press, 1958. Pp. 145-160.

Emrich, Wilhelm. *Franz Kafka*. Bonn: Athenäum-Verlag, 1958.

Flores, Angel. *Franz Kafka, A Chronology and Bibliography*. Houlton, Maine: Bern Porter, 1944.

— (ed.). *The Kafka Problem*. New York: New Directions, 1946.

— "The Art of Kafka," *Yale Review* (Winter, 1949), pp. 365-367.

Flores, Angel, and Swander, Homer. *Franz Kafka Today*.

Madison: The University of Wisconsin Press, 1958.

Flores, Kate. "Biographical Notes," *The Kafka Problem*, ed. A. Flores. New York: New Directions, 1946. Pp. 1-19.

Fuchs, Rudolf. "Social Awareness," *The Kafka Problem*, ed. A. Flores. New York: New Directions, 1946. Pp. 247-253.

Goodman, Paul. *Kafka's Prayer*. New York: Vanguard, 1947.

Gray, Ronald. *Kafka's Castle*. Cambridge: Cambridge University Press, 1956.

Groethuysen, Bernard. "Introduction," *Le Procès* [French translation of *Der Prozess*]. Paris: Gallimard, 1933.

— "The Endless Labyrinth," *The Kafka Problem*, ed. A. Flores. New York: New Directions, 1946. Pp. 376-390.

Hardt, Ludwig. "Recollections," *The Kafka Problem*, ed. A. Flores. New York: New Directions, 1946. Pp. 32-36.

Heller, Erich. *The Disinherited Mind*. Cambridge: Bowes and Bowes, 1952.

Hoffman, Frederick J. "Escape from Father," *The Kafka Problem*, ed. A. Flores. New York: New Directions, 1946. Pp. 214-246.

Hubben, William. *Four Prophets of Our Destiny: Kierkegaard, Dostoevsky, Nietzsche, Kafka*. New York: Macmillan, 1952,

Kelly, John. "Franz Kafka's *Trial* and the Theology of Crisis," *Southern Review* (Spring, 1940), pp. 748-766.

Landsberg, Paul L. "The Metamorphosis," *The Kafka Problem*, ed. A. Flores. New York: New Directions, 1946. Pp. 122-133.

Lerner, Max. "Franz Kafka and the Human Voyage," *Saturday Review of Literature* (June 7. 1941), pp. 3-4ff.

Mann, Thomas. "Homage," *The Castle*. New York: Knopf, 1941. Pp. v-xvi.

Muir, Edwin. "Introductory Note," *The Castle*. New York: Knopf, 1930. Pp. v-xi.

— "Introductory Note," *The Great Wall of China*. London: Secker, 1933.

— "Franz Kafka," *A Franz Kafka Miscellany*. New York: Twice a Year Press, 1940. Pp. 55-56.

Neider, Charles. *The Frozen Sea*. New York: Oxford University Press, 1948.

— "Kafka and the Cabalists," *Quarterly Review of Literature*, II, No. 3 (1945), pp. 250-262.

Pascal, Roy. *The German Novel*. Toronto: The University of Toronto Press, 1956.

Pearce, Donald. *"The Castle:* Kafka's Divine Comedy," *Franz Kafka Today*, ed. A. Flores. Madison: The University of Wisconsin Press, 1958. Pp. 165-172.

Poggioli, Renato. "Kafka and Dostoyevsky," *The Kafka Problem*, ed. A. Flores. New York: New Directions, 1946. Pp. 97-107.

Politzer, Heinz. "Franz Kafka's Letter to His Father," *Germanic Review*, XXVIII (October, 1953), pp. 165-179.

— "Prague and the Origins of R. M. Rilke, F. Kafka and F. Werfel," *Modern Language Quarterly*, XVI, No. 1 (March, 1955).

— *Franz Kafka: Parable and Paradox*. Ithaca: Cornell University Press, 1962.

Rahv, Philip. "The Hero as Lonely Man," *The Kenyon Review* (Winter, 1939), pp. 60-74.

Reiss, H. S. *Franz Kafka, eine Betrachtung seines Werkes*. Heidelberg: Verlag Lambert Schneider, 1956.

Rochefort, Robert. *Kafka; ou, L'irréductible espoir*. Paris: R. Julliard, 1947.

Savage, D. S. "Franz Kafka: Faith and Vocation," *The Kafka Problem*, ed. A. Flores. New York: New Directions, 1946. Pp. 319-336.

Schoeps, Hans Joachim. "The Tragedy of Faithlessness," *The Kafka Problem*, ed. A. Flores. New York: New Directions, 1946. Pp. 287-297.

116

Slochower, Harry. "Franz Kafka, Pre-Fascist Exile," *A Franz Kafka Miscellany*. New York: Twice a Year Press, 1940. Pp. 7-30.

Spaini, Alberto. "The Trial," *The Kafka Problem*, ed. A. Flores. New York: New Directions, 1946. Pp. 143-150.

Stumpf, W. "Franz Kafka," *Literarische Revue*, III (1949), pp. 281-283.

Tauber, Herbert. *Franz Kafka, eine Deutung seiner Werke*. Zurich: Oprecht Verlag, 1941.

Uyttersprot, Herman. *Zur Struktur Kafkas "Der Prozess."* Brussels: Marcel Didier, 1953.

Vietta, Egon. "Franz Kafka und unsere Zeit," *Neue Schweizer Rundschau*, XXIV (July, 1931), pp. 565-577.

Wagenbach, Klaus. *Franz Kafka. Eine Biographie seiner Jugend, 1883 bis 1912*. Verlag Francke Bern, 1958.

Wahl, Jean. "Kierkegaard and Kafka," *The Kafka Problem*, ed. A. Flores. New York: New Directions, 1946. Pp. 262-275.

Warren, Austin. "Kosmos Kafka," *Southern Review* (Autumn, 1941), pp. 350-365.

— *Rage for Order*. Chicago: The University of Chicago Press, 1948.

Weidlé, Wladimir. "The Negative Capability," *The Kafka Problem*, ed. A. Flores. New York: New Directions, 1946. Pp. 354-362.

Werfel, Franz. "Recollections," *The Kafka Problem*, ed. A. Flores. New York: New Directions, 1946. P. 37.

West, Rebecca. *The Court and the Castle*. New Haven: Yale University Press, 1957.

Wilson, Edmund. *Classics and Commercials*. New York: Farrar, Straus and Co., 1950.

Winkler, R. O. C. "The Three Novels," *The Kafka Problem*, ed. A. Flores. New York: New Directions, 1946. Pp. 192-198.

117

Works by Albert Camus (in chronological order)

Révolte dans les Asturies: Essai de création collective.
Alger: Charlot, 1936.
L'Envers et l'Endroit. Alger: Charlot, 1937. Reprinted
Paris: Gallimard, 1957 and 1958.
Noces. Alger: Charlot, 1938.
L'Etranger (Récit). Paris: Gallimard, 1942. Translated
by Stuart Gilbert. New York: Alfred A. Knopf,
1946.
Le Mythe de Sisyphe. Paris: Gallimard, 1942. Translated
by Justin O'Brien. New York: Alfred A. Knopf,
1955.
Lettres à un ami allemand. Paris: Gallimard, 1945.
Le Malentendu et Caligula. Paris: Gallimard, 1944.
Translated by Stuart Gilbert. Norfolk, Con-
necticut: New Directions, 1948.
La Peste (Chronique). Paris: Gallimard, 1947. Translated
by Stuart Gilbert. New York: Alfred A. Knopf,
1948.
L'Etat de Siège. Paris: Gallimard, 1948.
Les Justes. Paris: Gallimard, 1950. Translated by Elizabeth
Sprigge and Philip Warner. Microfilm, 1957.
Actuelles I. Paris: Gallimard, 1950.
L'Homme révolté. Paris: Gallimard, 1951. Translated by
Anthony Bower. New York: Alfred A. Knopf,
1954.
Actuelles II. Paris: Gallimard, 1953.
L'Eté. Paris: Gallimard, 1954.
La Chute (Récit). Paris: Gallimard, 1956. Translated by
Justin O'Brien. New York: Alfred A. Knopf, 1957.
L'Exil et le Royaume. Paris: Gallimard, 1957. Translated
by Justin O'Brien. New York: Alfred A. Knopf, 1958.
*Speech of Acceptance upon the Award of the Nobel Prize for
Literature.* Translated by Justin O'Brien. New
York: Alfred A. Knopf, 1958.
Carnets. Paris: Gallimard, 1962.

118

Criticism of Camus' Work

"Absurdiste," *The New Yorker*, XXII, No. 22 (April 20, 1946), p. 22.

Bieber, Konrad. *"Engagement* as a Professional Risk," *Yale French Studies*, No. 16 (Winter, 1955-1956), pp. 29-39.

Bonnier, Henry. *Albert Camus ou la force d'être*. Lyon: E. Vitte, 1959.

Brée, Germaine. *Camus*. New Brunswick: Rutgers University Press, 1959.

— "Introduction to Albert Camus," *French Studies*, No. 4 (January, 1950), pp. 27-37.

Brée, Germaine, and Guiton, Margaret. *An Age of Fiction: The French Novel from Gide to Camus*. New Brunswick: Rutgers University Press, 1957.

Brombert, Victor. "Camus and the Novel of the 'Absurd,'" *Yale French Studies*, No. 1 (Spring-Summer, 1948), pp. 119-123.

Chiaromonte, Nicola. "Sartre versus Camus: A Political Quarrel," *Partisan Review*, LXX, No. 6 (November-December, 1952), pp. 680-686.

Cruikshank, J. "Camus' Technique in *L'Etranger*," *French Studies* (Autumn, 1955).

Fowlie, Wallace. "The French Literary Mind," *Accent*, VIII, No. 2 (Winter, 1948), pp. 67-81.

Frohock, W. M. "Camus: Image, Influence and Sensibility," *Yale French Studies*, II, No. 2 (Fourth Study), pp. 91-99.

Galtier-Boisser, Jean (directeur). *Dictionnaire des contemporains, Crapouillet No. 8*. Paris: 1951.

Gershman, Herbert S. "On *L'Etranger*," *French Review*, IX, No. 4 (February, 1956), pp. 299-305.

Hanna, Thomas. *The Thought and Art of Albert Camus*. Chicago: Henry Regnery Co., 1958.

John, S. "Image and Symbol in the Work of Albert Camus," *French Studies*, IX, No. 1 (January, 1955), pp. 493-497.

Luppé, Robert de. *Albert Camus*. Paris: Presses Universitaires, 1951.

"Man in a Vacuum," *Time* (May 20, 1946), p. 92.

Maquet, Albert. *Albert Camus ou l'invincible été*. Paris: Editions Debresse, 1955.

Peyre, Henri. "The Resistance and Literary Revival in France," *Yale Review*, XXXV, No. 1 (September, 1945), pp. 84-92.

Picon, Gaetan. *Panorama de la nouvelle littérature française*. Paris: Gallimard, 1949.

Quillot, Roger. *La Mer et les prisons: Essai sur Albert Camus*. Paris: Gallimard, 1956.

Rolo, Charles. "Albert Camus: A Good Man," *The Atlantic* (May, 1958), pp. 27-33.

Sartre, Jean-Paul. "Explication de *L'Etranger*," *Cahiers du Sud* (Février, 1943). (Typewritten.)

— *Literary and Philosophical Essays*. Translated by Annette Michelson. London: Rider and Co., 1955.

Spiegelberg, Herbert. "French Existentialism: Its Social Philosophies," *Kenyon Review*, XVI, No. 3 (Summer 1954), pp. 446-462.

Thody, Philip. *Albert Camus: A Study of His Work*. London: Hamish Hamilton, 1957.

Viggiani, Carl A. "Camus' *L'Etranger*," *Publications of the Modern Language Association*, No. 5 (December, 1956), pp. 865-887.

Other Sources

Bibliography of Critical and Bibliographical References for the Study of Contemporary French Literature. New York: Stechert-Hafner, Inc.

Columbia Dictionary of Modern European Literature. New York: Columbia University Press, 1947.

D'Astorg, Bertrand. *Aspects de la littérature européenne depuis 1945*. Paris: Ed. du Seuil, 1952.

120

UNIVERSITY OF NORTH CAROLINA
STUDIES IN THE GERMANIC LANGUAGES
AND LITERATURES

1. Herbert W. Reichert. THE BASIC CONCEPTS IN THE PHILOSOPHY OF GOTT-FRIED KELLER. 1949. Pp. 164. Out of print.
2. Olga Marx and Ernst Morwitz. THE WORKS OF STEFAN GEORGE. Rendered into English. 1949. Out of print.
3. Paul H. Curts. HEROD AND MARIAMNE, A Tragedy in Five Acts by Friedrich Hebbel, Translated into English Verse. 1950. Pp. 96. Out of print.
4. Frederic E. Coenen. FRANZ GRILLPARZER'S PORTRAITURE OF MEN. 1951. Pp. xii, 135. Out of print.
5. Edwin H. Zeydel and B. Q. Morgan. THE PARZIVAL OF WOLFRAM VON ESCHEN-BACH. Translated into English Verse, with Introductions, Notes, and Connecting Summaries. 1951, 1956, 1960. Pp. xii, 370. Paper $4.50.
6. James C. O'Flaherty. UNITY AND LANGUAGE: A STUDY IN THE PHILOSOPHY OF JOHANN GEORG HAMANN. 1952. Out of print.
7. Sten G. Flygt. FRIEDRICH HEBBEL'S CONCEPTION OF MOVEMENT IN THE ABSOLUTE AND IN HISTORY. 1952. Out of print.
8. Richard Kuehnemund. ARMINIUS OR THE RISE OF A NATIONAL SYMBOL. (From Hutten to Grabbe.) 1953. Pp. xxx, 122. Cloth $3.50.
9. Lawrence S. Thompson. WILHELM WAIBLINGER IN ITALY. 1953. Pp. ix, 105. Paper $3.00.
10. Frederick Hiebel. NOVALIS. GERMAN POET - EUROPEAN THINKER - CHRISTIAN MYSTIC. 1953. Pp. xii, 126. 2nd rev. ed. 1959. Paper $3.50.
11. Walter Silz. Realism and Reality: Studies in the German Novelle of Poetic Realism. 1954. Third printing, 1962. Fourth printing, 1966. Pp. xiv, 168. Cloth $5.50.
12. Percy Matenko. LUDWIG TIECK AND AMERICA. 1954. Out of print.
13. Wilhelm Dilthey. THE ESSENCE OF PHILOSOPHY. Rendered into English by Stephen A. Emery and William T. Emery. 1954, 1961. Pp. xii, 78. Paper $1.50.
14. Edwin H. Zeydel and B. Q. Morgan. GREGORIUS. A Medieval Oedipus Legend by Hartmann von Aue. Translated in Rhyming Couplets with Introduction and Notes. 1955. Out of print.
15. Alfred G. Steer, Jr. GOETHE'S SOCIAL PHILOSOPHY AS REVEALED IN CAMPAGNE IN FRANKREICH AND BELAGERUNG VON MAINZ, With three full-page illustrations. 1955. Pp. xiv, 178. Paper $4.00.
16. Edwin H. Zeydel. GOETHE THE LYRIST. 100 Poems in New Translations facing the Original Texts. With a Biographical Introduction and an Appendix on Musical Settings. 1955. Pp. xviii, 182. 2nd ed. 1958. 3rd printing, 1966. Cloth $4.00.
17. Hermann J. Weigand. THREE CHAPTERS ON COURTLY LOVE IN ARTHURIAN FRANCE AND GERMANY. Out of print.
18. George Fenwick Jones. WITTENWILER'S „RING" AND THE ANONYMOUS SCOTS POEM „COLKELBIE SOW". Two Comic-Didactic Works from the Fifteenth Century. Translated into English. With five illustrations. 1956. Pp. xiv, 246. Paper $4.50.
19. George C. Schoolfield. THE FIGURE OF THE MUSICIAN IN GERMAN LITERATURE. 1956. Out of print.
20. Edwin H. Zeydel. POEMS OF GOETHE. A Sequel to GOETHE THE LYRIST. New Translations facing the Originals. With an Introduction and a List of Musical Settings. 1957. Pp. xii, 126. Paper $3.25. Out of print.
21. Joseph Mileck. HERMANN HESSE AND HIS CRITICS. The Criticism and Bibliography of Half a Century. 1958. Out of print.
22. Ernest N. Kirrmann. DEATH AND THE PLOWMAN or THE BOHEMIAN PLOWMAN. A Disputatious and Consolatory Dialogue about Death from the Year 1400. Translated from the Modern German Version of Alois Bernt. 1958. Pp. xviii, 40. Paper $1.85.
23. Edwin H. Zeydel. RUODLIEB, THE EARLIEST COURTLY NOVEL (after 1050). Introduction, Text, Translation, Commentary, and Textual Notes. With seven illustrations. 1959. Second printing, 1963. Pp. xii, 165. Paper $4.50.
24. John T. Krumpelmann. THE MAIDEN OF ORLEANS. A Romantic Tragedy in Five Acts by Friedrich Schiller. Translated into English in the Verse Forms of the Original German. 1959. Out of print. [See volume 37, page ii of this volume.]
25. George Fenwick Jones. HONOR IN GERMAN LITERATURE. 1959. Pp. xii, 208. Paper $4.50.
26. MIDDLE AGES—REFORMATION—VOLKSKUNDE. FESTSCHRIFT for John G. Kunstmann. Twenty Essays. 1959. Out of Print.
27. Martin Dyck. NOVALIS AND MATHEMATICS. 1960. Pp. xii, 109. Paper $3.50.
28. Claude Hill and Ralph Ley. THE DRAMA OF GERMAN EXPRESSIONISM. A German-English Bibliography. 1960. Pp. xii, 211. Paper $5.00. Out of print.
29. George S. Schoolfield. THE GERMAN LYRIC OF THE BAROQUE IN ENGLISH TRANSLATION. 1961. Pp. x, 380. Paper $7.00.